Lancaster Castle

Please be aware that for most of its history, Lancaster Castle has served as a prison and courthouse. As a result, most of its history has been associated with law and order, crime and punishment.
These topics therefore form the major part of this book; themes treated include prisons and imprisonment, physical punishment and capital punishment (including hanging).

In memory of Karen

First published in 2024
by Palatine Books
Carnegie House
Chatsworth Road
Lancaster LA1 4SL
www.palatinebooks.com

Copyright © Colin Penny and Ann-Marie Michel

All rights reserved
Unauthorised duplication contravenes existing laws

The right of Colin Penny and Ann-Marie Michel
to be identified as the authors of this work has been asserted in
accordance with the Copyright, Designs and Patents act 1988

British Library Cataloguing-in-Publication data
A catalogue record for this book is available from the
British Library

Paperback ISBN 13: 978-1-910837-50-4

Designed and typeset by Carnegie Book Production
www.carnegiebookproduction.com

Printed and bound by Zenith

A Guide

to

LANCASTER CASTLE

for the

Young and Curious

Colin Penny and Ann-Marie Michel

Contents

Welcome	1
The Gatehouse	3
A New Modern Prison	7
The Governor's House	11
The Witches' Tower	13
The King's Evidence Tower	17
The Male and Female Felons' Towers	21
The Keep	23
'A' Wing and the Silent System	31
The Debtors' Wing	35
The Female Penitentiary	41
Prison Work	45
Prison Food	51
Hadrian's Tower	55
Transportation to the Colonies	59
The Old Cells	63
The Shire Hall	67
The Library	73
The Crown Court	79
The Drop Room	83
The Grand Jury Room	87
The Duke of Lancaster	91
Lancaster Castle in the modern age	95
Biography	103
Timeline	105
Glossary	109
Punishment	114
Image credits	117

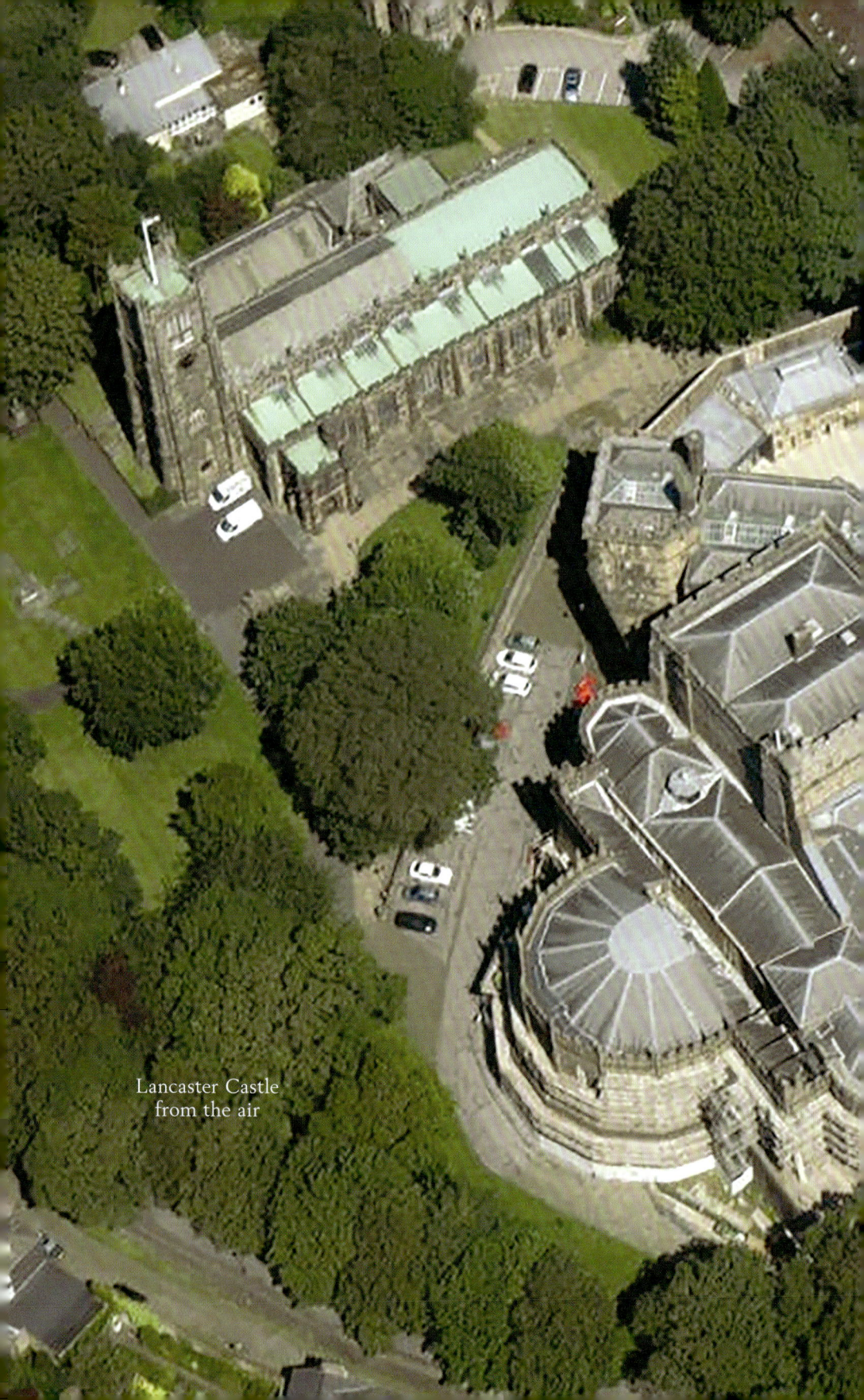

Lancaster Castle from the air

Welcome

Now who might you be and what are you doing in my castle? Well ... it's not exactly mine – it belongs to the King right enough – but from 1784 to 1834, I was governor of the prison here at Lancaster Castle, so I reckon that makes me some kind of boss. I might be a little less solid these days – I mean, some people can't even see me! – but I still like haunting the corridors. My name is John Higgin Jnr, and my father, who was also called John Higgin, was governor here before me, so you see, I spent over fifty years here, more time than most prisoners. Goodness me, I've seen some changes! But still, my fifty years is nothing when you think that this castle is over 900 years old ... And then there are the people – oh, I could tell you a thing or two about the rogues who were here, and I don't just mean the prisoners. In fact, come to think of it, there's probably a shady ghost or two still hanging around here – like me. But no need to worry, we're all friendly enough. In fact, we like to show off the place. Why don't you join me for a trip through history as we explore some of the most interesting corners of this old place and some of the exciting stories of Lancaster Castle? I'll let you out when we're finished – promise.

Look above you: John O'Gaunt stands sentry over the gate

The Gatehouse

So, let's start here, where you came in. In medieval times, the gatehouse was one of the most important parts of the castle. It was the entrance, the very first thing visitors would see – so you wanted to make an impression. The more impressive the gatehouse, the more important – and rich! – the owner of the castle would look. The gatehouse you see today was built in 1405 by Henry, Prince of Wales, who was the son of King Henry IV. Not surprising then that it is so magnificent – it was built by a royal family, who could afford to spend a huge amount of money to get the best gatehouse around. It is called the 'John O'Gaunt gatehouse'. John O'Gaunt was the second Duke of Lancaster, and the father of Henry IV. Just above the gate you can see a statue of him that was put there in 1822, and on either side, the shield of his son Henry IV, and his grandson, Henry, Prince of Wales. This gatehouse is actually built around an even earlier one, made by King John in 1210.

The handle turns the cogs, which pull the chain, which raises the portcullis

Come closer!
Let me spew boiling oil on you

But the entrance wasn't just about making an impression. There was something else to consider ... defence. The entrance was always going to be a weak spot in the castle's defences, so it had to be protected. This gatehouse is 20 metres high with a massive iron portcullis which could be lowered in front of the gates once they were shut. It has arrow slits, so hidden archers could fire on any attackers. Anyone who managed to fight their way through that still had to get past what were called 'murder holes' – if you look up, you'll see them. They look like horrible faces with huge open mouths. Defending soldiers on the roof could pour boiling oil, or tar, or even just water through these holes onto their

Can you spot the murder holes?

enemies below. How's that for a warm welcome?

Inside the gatehouse are six huge rooms. These were used as living space for the constable, who looked after the castle, and as offices. In my day, we used these rooms for prisoners — some for debtors, and others for prisoners whose crimes weren't too serious. We always tried to keep petty criminals away from more serious offenders. If you look at the pictures, you can see some drawings of the debtors' rooms as they were in my time.

One of the debtors' rooms in the gatehouse

Implements used in foiled escape attempts ... wonder what happened to the other half of the scissors?

A New Modern Prison

COME ALONG THROUGH THE GATEHOUSE NOW; there's more space here in this courtyard. Nice view too – but you might notice that some of these buildings don't look quite as old as the medieval part we just looked at. Well, that's because Lancaster Castle has been modernised. In 1774 a man called John Howard, who was a wealthy man from Bedfordshire, visited the castle. He had become very concerned about the conditions in English prisons and he was determined to do something about it! He wanted to make things better – so he spent his life travelling around the country inspecting prisons and writing reports about them which he sent to the government. He had a lot of ideas about how things could be improved. You see, at that time prisons were very different. To start with, there were very few cells. Instead, prisoners were usually kept all together. At night they slept in big rooms called dormitories, and they spent their time in equally large dayrooms during the day. Men, women and children were mixed in together and it made it near impossible to keep any kind of order. There was hardly any healthcare, very poor hygiene, no heating, the food was terrible, there weren't enough beds – it was chaos. In some cases, you even had to pay rent for your cell, for example if you were waiting for your trial. And if you couldn't

The courtyard then and now. Can you find the clock tower, the cloister walk, and the medieval keep?

pay the bill, then you couldn't leave – even if you'd been found not guilty!

Now I know what you're thinking – why didn't the governor take control? Well, governors like me weren't paid any money for doing the job – but a man will make his wage one way or another, by charging rent for cells, and even by running a pub in the prison (known as the Tap) where prisoners with money could buy a drink. Governors also made deals with the merchants providing the food and other things brought into the prison. Can you imagine it? Hundreds of people mixed together in filthy conditions, many of them drunk, arguing, fighting, chattering – and disease was a constant problem, not just for the prisoners but for the turnkeys and even governors like me. Take it from me, it was no easy job trying to keep order. In fact, many prisoners left even worse than they had come in, because the younger prisoners soon learned new tricks from the older ones. John Howard said this disgraceful state of affairs could not go on, and eventually Parliament agreed. They passed a number of reform acts designed to clean up prisons and create some kind of order through separation and discipline – you know, rules and regulations.

Why was a turnkey called a turnkey?

The Governor's House, where my family and I lived. Keep off the garden!

The Governor's House

Now here's a bit of the castle that I know really well ... next to the gatehouse is my house. It was built in 1788, and I was the first person to live in it with my family. Before that we lived a short distance from the castle in what is now called the Judges' Lodgings – that's because when we moved out, the judges moved in!

It was decided, though, that it would be better if the governor of the prison lived inside, so that they would be on the spot if they were needed – not much chance of a day off, then. Still, living in this house had its good points – it had plenty of room and was quite comfortable. We even had a garden with roses and other flowers which were looked after by some of the prisoners. I used to let prisoners who had been ill walk or sit in it after their release from the hospital if they were still too weak to work. The garden was also a useful way to physically separate the criminals from the other prisoners – they each had their cell blocks on opposite sides of it. And the house is well-placed, too. From here I could see pretty much the whole prison – especially from the top floor – notice how the windows on the central tower look out in all directions. I lived here with my wife and my son, Thomas, who worked as my assistant.

Waiter, there's a witch in my well

The Witches' Tower

Now this tower actually has two names ... most people call it the Witches' Tower because the Lancashire Witches are said to have been imprisoned in the dungeon underneath it – but I'll tell you more about them later. But it was also called 'The Well Tower' because there is a very deep well inside which used to provide some of the drinking water for the people living and working here. Access to water is very important for a castle. Just think about it – if the castle was attacked or besieged, then those inside could be cut off from the River Lune, or any other source of water, for a very long time ... and if there was no water supply inside the building ... well, you'd be getting mighty thirsty. How long do you think you could last? Without water, the castle would have had to surrender after only a few days. I've heard that there could be as many as fourteen wells inside the building, but you can't see them because most of them have now been built over.

Whatever you call it, this tower was built in about 1340, probably because in 1322 the king of Scotland, Robert the Bruce, attacked

Robert Bruce, burner of castle, town and county

Come on in! Dungeon's lovely

the castle and the town of Lancaster. He and his army did a lot of damage, so when it was over, this tower was built to strengthen the castle's defences — so that they wouldn't get caught out again. It's possible that another tower, which in my day was called the Dungeon Tower, was built at the same time as the Witches' Tower. No prizes for guessing why we called it the Dungeon Tower! Yes, we kept prisoners in there — and it was really awful. I'll tell you more about that later, but let's just say I was very glad when it was emptied and pulled down in 1818 to make room for the Female Penitentiary.

So these towers were originally built for defence. They stood in front of the castle walls so that arrows could be fired from all sides against any attackers. The wall that you can see now on either side of the Witches' Tower came much later — in fact, it was built in my time.

Soldiers probably lived in the tower when it was first built, but by the time I came here it was being used to hold debtors. If you look at the pictures, you can see what the rooms looked like in my day and how they have changed.

The dungeon, though, is still a terrible place. It's underground, so there's no light at all. It's damp at the best of times, but when it rains the water runs right down the walls. All that damp has made them turn green. It's also very cold, even in summer. And see those big iron rings in the floor? It's said that people imprisoned there who were waiting for their trial, like the Lancashire Witches, were chained to them. Horrible! Not surprisingly, some of them died down there. And they hadn't even been found guilty yet! In fact, some were probably innocent ... gives me shivers just thinking about it. Come on – let's get out of here.

A ring for the shackles

Neither witches nor riches – debtors in the Well Tower

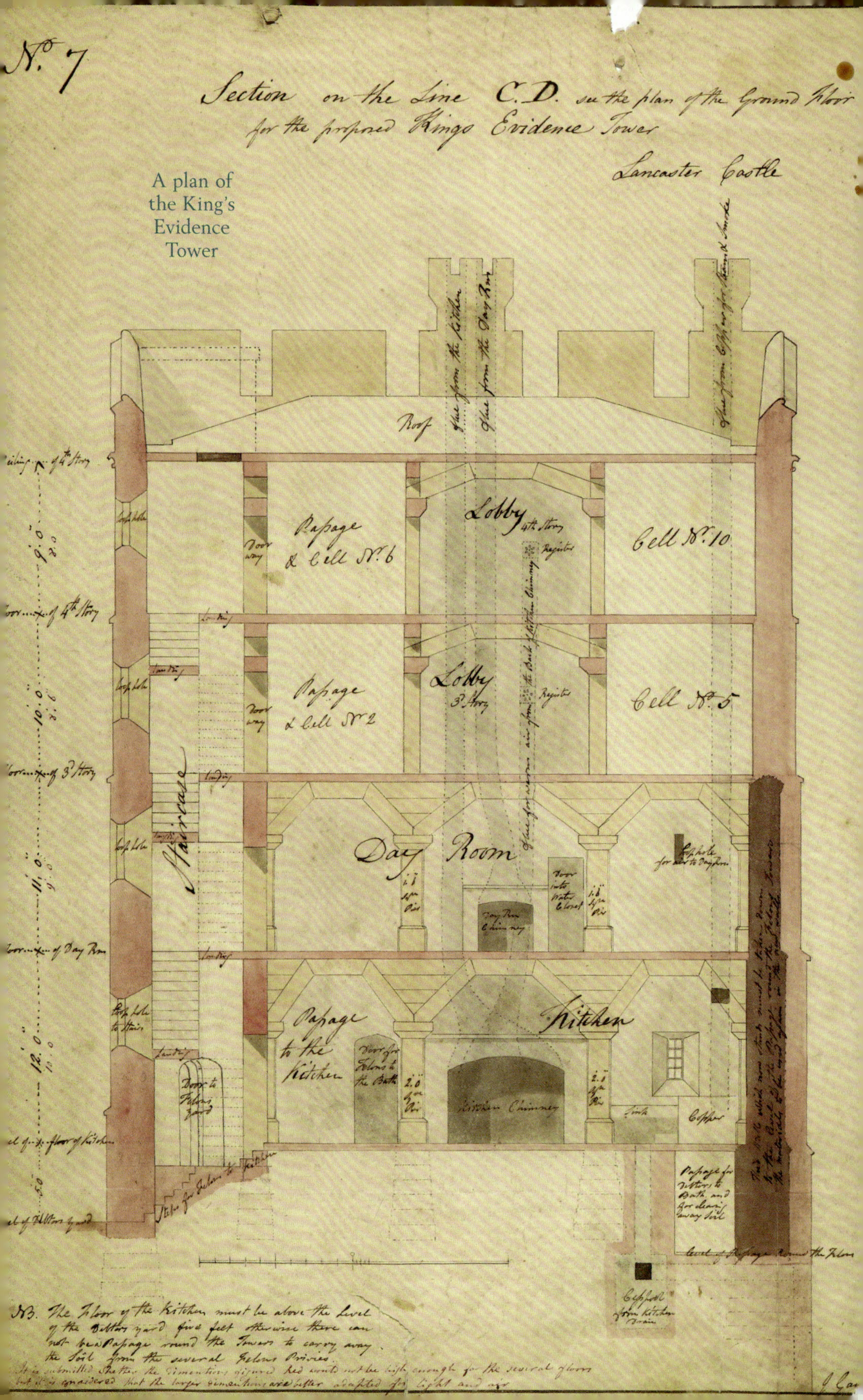

N.º 7

Section on the Line C.D. see the plan of the Ground Floor for the proposed Kings Evidence Tower

Lancaster Castle

A plan of the King's Evidence Tower

Roof

Passage & Cell N.º 6 | Lobby 4th Story | Cell N.º 10

Passage & Cell N.º 2 | Lobby 3rd Story | Cell N.º 5

Staircase | Day Room

Passage to the Kitchen | Kitchen

NB. The Floor of the Kitchen must be above the Level of the Felons yard five feet otherwise there can not be a Passage round the Tower to carry away the Soil from the several Felons Privies.
It is submitted whether the Dimensions figured hereon would not be high enough for the several floors but it is considered that the larger Dimensions are better adapted for Light and air

The King's Evidence Tower

NOW THIS TOWER WAS BUILT a bit later than some of the others, but to be honest I'm not right sure of the date ... when you've been here as long as I have, you can't remember everything! I do remember, though, that in 1812 we used to call it 'the new tower', so I reckon that means it was probably built around 1810. It's called the King's Evidence Tower.

What does King's Evidence mean? Well, back in my day we didn't have any of your fancy fingerprints or forensic science to prove that a person had committed a crime. In most trials, it was just one person's word against another's, and the jury had to decide who they believed the most. Sometimes there might be other evidence ... you might find stolen goods in a person's home, for example. But a lot of the time there just wasn't much to go on.

However, some crimes — like forging fake banknotes — were committed by groups of people, rather than just one individual. So if the constables managed to arrest a gang, then they could try to 'persuade' one or more of them to 'turn King's Evidence' on the others in exchange for their freedom. Quite a few of 'em did too ... well, it's not surprising. No honour among thieves, so they say. And what's more, in my day, there were 220 crimes that carried the death penalty, so if you'd been caught, you were in a right fix! To make matters worse, most defendants couldn't afford a defence lawyer – no chance. So you see why some of them chose this option to avoid prison or even the noose.

Then they would have to go into the courtroom and give evidence for the prosecution, sometimes even against their friends, which would almost certainly lead to a guilty verdict. Of course, once they had agreed to do this, it wasn't safe to keep them with the other

Pickpocketing – a scourge of society

prisoners, in case they changed their minds, or even were attacked ... they wouldn't be very popular, now would they? So this tower was built to accommodate them. And just to show the King's appreciation, the cells here are actually much nicer than a lot of the others — these folk even had their very own fireplace.

The King's Evidence Tower had all the mod cons. And, by the twentieth century, a natty colour scheme, as prisoners were taught painting and decorating skills here

Felons this way

The Male and Female Felons' Towers

REMEMBER I TOLD YOU how John Howard got Parliament to make some new rules to modernise prisons? Well, that's why we have this tower, and another just like it which is now part of 'A' wing. These towers were designed by Thomas Harrison and built in 1793. They were five floors high, with eight cells on each floor. These cells were very modern, and they allowed me to separate the male prisoners into groups based on things such as their type of crime, or how well-behaved they were, or their length of sentence. In this way, I could try and stop the prisoners who I thought *maybe* could be reformed from meeting those who definitely were trouble – repeat offenders and the like. At the same time a similar tower, on three floors, was built for female felons on the other side of the castle. To stop the men and women meeting each other, a wall was built between them.

Inside the male felons' tower

CASTLE The Keep: the oldest part of the castle

The Keep

IMPRESSIVE, ISN'T IT? This is the oldest part of the castle, and it was built around 1150 – that's nearly 900 years ago!

The first castle was built even earlier, in 1093, by a man called Roger de Poitou. He was a Norman, which means he came from Normandy – today that's a part of France, but back then it was an independent area ruled by a duke. In 1066, the Normans invaded England and killed the king, Harold II, at the Battle of Hastings. They were led by Duke William, who became known as William the Conqueror.

Two years later, our boy Roger (who was only about ten years old at the time) travelled to England with his father. When he grew up, he helped the Normans conquer the north of England and was rewarded with a new title – Lord of the Honour of Lancaster. Of course, honour is all well and good – but a huge amount of land to go with it is even better. So lucky Roger built a new castle on top of this hill to protect his new lands.

Roger immortalised in a stained-glass window at Lancaster Priory

The castle keep, on the right-hand side. See the wide steps leading up to the entrance

A view of Lancaster in 1868, with Morecambe Bay in the background

It's a very good spot to build a castle, on top of a steep hill ... you can see for miles around, especially if you build a very high tower on top of that.

It's especially important that from the top of the Keep you can see right across Morecambe Bay, because back in the eleventh century that is the way the Scots would have come if they were going to attack – they would cross the Bay at low tide. You see, at that time, the English border with Scotland was much closer than it is today – it was only about ten miles away – so trouble with the Scots was always a very real threat.

The first castle was probably made of wood, and would have been a tower surrounded by a fence – known as a 'motte and bailey' castle.

The wooden castle lasted for about 55 years, when it was replaced by the one you see today. It wasn't actually built by the Normans, though – it was built by the Scots because at that time they controlled the north west of

England. King David I of Scotland (1124–53) was a great castle-builder in stone, and it was he who replaced the wooden tower with this magnificent keep. It's 24 metres long, 24 metres wide and 21 metres high – and in case you're wondering, the walls are about 3 metres thick.

When it was built, though, it wasn't quite so tall as it is now – it stood only about 17 metres high. The top floor was added in 1585. At this time many castles around the English coast were strengthened because it was feared that the Spanish would invade ... something they attempted three years later, in 1588. Luckily, they were prevented by the defeat of the Spanish Armada.

Inside the Keep, there is a wall running through the middle which divides the space into two – a north side and a south side. No records have survived telling

Inside the vast, vaulted Keep

us what the rooms were used for, but at least one huge hall would have been used by the owner of the castle to hold court and host banquets for visitors. Smaller spaces would have been used for bedrooms, a chapel, servants' quarters and a kitchen. By the mid-eighteenth century, the Keep contained the 'Shire Hall', which was used by judges to hear civil cases. These cases were not serious enough to be considered criminal – usually people arguing about who owned land, or wrongs that had been done to them. At the same time another part of the Keep was being used to hold people who were mentally ill. These people had done nothing wrong – but at the time, the authorities had nowhere else to send them, other than the local prison. This terrible practice ended in 1816 when Lancaster Moor Hospital was built.

The entrance to the Keep wasn't originally on the ground floor. It was actually on the first floor and there was a flight of steps up to it – like in the picture you can see on page 25. The Keep had to be strong because at the time it was built, it was the castle's last line of defence. If an enemy managed to get inside the walls, all surviving defenders would run for the Keep: up the steps, though the door, and bolt it shut behind them. Safe! At least for a while.

The Keep would have been well stocked with food and water. The door would have been very thick and strong, and also quite narrow. Attackers would have to go up the flight of steps, one behind the other, whilst defenders rained rocks and stones down upon their heads from the rooftop. Then they would have to break down the door – and even then, they could only get in one at a time. So in theory, a very small number of defenders could hold back a much larger force.

But the attackers were clever. They found a way around this problem. What they did was not bother trying to get through the door at all. Instead, they would dig an underground tunnel to one of the corners of the keep. Then they would dig a huge hole underneath that corner. They reinforced the hole with tree trunks which they cut down locally, and once it was big enough, they would stuff it full of as much wood, fat and other flammable material as they could find. Then they would set fire to it, run back down their tunnel and wait outside. As the fire raged underground it would burn through the tree trunks that were holding up the roof, and eventually the roof – and the hole – would collapse. When it did, the corner of the keep above the hole would collapse too – and at that point, the attackers could get in. This never happened at Lancaster as the castle was rarely attacked, and when it was, it tended to give up without a fight – although there were exceptions!

In the modern, twentieth-century prison, the Keep had a variety of uses including classrooms for prisoner education, offices, a chapel and a gymnasium.

Masked prisoners in their daily drudge

'A' Wing and the Silent System

THIS IS ONE OF THE MORE 'modern' prison buildings here at Lancaster Castle. It was built in about 1871, and the design is known as the 'Pentonville Style'. Pentonville Prison is in London, and this type of prison block was first used there – long rows of cells all running in a straight line.

It was built at a time when something called the 'Silent System' was being used in many prisons in Britain. Can you guess what that meant? Yes, that's right – NO TALKING! I mean not a peep! Can you imagine that?
Not being allowed to talk at all unless you were given permission by a turnkey? It seems pretty harsh now, but at that time, people were worried that not enough prisoners were actually sorry for what they had done. They believed prison was seen as an inconvenience – an interruption in a criminal's 'career' of crime. Having been caught, criminals would 'do their time' and then just pick up where they left off when they got out. In other words, prison would achieve nothing, because criminals would not change their ways. So drastic action was needed. And one of the ideas they came up with was the silent system. If prisoners were allowed to chatter away to each other, then how

could they concentrate on what they were *supposed* to be thinking about whilst in prison – their own bad behaviour? Better to keep silent and think about how they ended up here. So by not allowing prisoners to talk, and keeping them alone in their cells at night with nothing else to do but think, eventually their conscience would kick in. They would start to examine their lives and their behaviour – and eventually realise that they had to change their ways. In other words, they would be sorry for what they had done. This was an important part of a prisoner's rehabilitation.

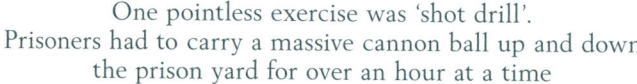

Zip it!

Now there was no time off for good behaviour in the silent system. Prisoners were not even allowed to talk whilst they were exercising in the prison yard. When I say exercise, I don't mean what you lot might mean ... things like playing football, cricket or hockey. Oh no, none of THAT. Exercise in prison meant walking slowly all around the main courtyard, again and again, just walking in circles ... and keeping silent whilst you were at it, of course. But even that wasn't strict enough. What if prisoners tried to signal to one another without actually speaking? Can't have that either. So prisoners were made

One pointless exercise was 'shot drill'.
Prisoners had to carry a massive cannon ball up and down the prison yard for over an hour at a time

An idealised picture of the headgear in use.

to wear a kind of leather hat which had a very long peak that came right down over their faces. Kind of a cross between a knight's helmet and a baseball cap, but you would need two holes cut in it so you could see where you were going. With everyone dressed in the same prison uniform, and their faces all covered up in these weird hats, it would be impossible to find a friend or an enemy, much less get a message to them.

So did all that silence work? That would be a deafening "No". It was impossible to stop prisoners finding ways to communicate, so it was all a bit pointless in the end. Neither did it seem to have much effect on whether or not a prisoner felt sorry for what they had done. But what it *did* do was make people ill. People need to communicate for their own mental health, and many – too many – were driven mad by being kept in total silence. Put pressure on the prison doctors and infirmaries too, and let's not forget, prisoners who are ill cannot work. So what's the good of that? By the early twentieth century, the whole idea was dropped and the silent system died a quiet death – at least here in Britain.

A similar, sinister, silent-system set-up

The Debtors' Wing today

The Debtors' Wing

NOW YOU MAY NOT KNOW what a debtor is, but trust me, it's simple. A debtor is someone who owes money to another person. The one who wants the money back is the creditor. So if I lent a penny to one of you young scamps (and I wouldn't, for I'm nobody's fool), I would be the creditor and you would be the debtor. You could only get 'out of debt' once you paid back the penny you owed me.

Today, it is rare for someone to be put in prison for owing money. It usually only happens to people who don't pay their taxes, but back in my day it was very different ... any creditor could have a person who owed them money sent to prison. The prisons that they were sent to were known as 'debtors' prisons', and two hundred years ago during the Industrial Revolution, debtors' prisons were full.

It was a time when someone with a good idea for a new business might be able to make a fortune, if they could only get it started. The problem was that many of these people had great ideas – but no money. So they needed to persuade someone to let them borrow it, either a bank or a wealthy individual. They would agree to pay the money back, with a little extra for the lender's trouble. This was called 'interest', and it had to be paid by a certain date. All would be fine if the new business did well. The owner would make enough money to pay back his debt and the business would grow.

But sometimes it didn't work out that way. Businesses did not do well, and then the debtor would not be able to pay the money back. They'd be in a right mess!

So you see, lending money could be a very risky business. That's why the government passed a number of laws (known as Debtors' Acts) to make debtors think twice about not paying.

Now you may be wondering, what's the point? If a person couldn't pay their debts on the outside, how could they ever pay if they were locked up? Well, the thing is, some people who owed money *could* have paid it back — they had the dosh. But they just refused to. Maybe they disagreed about the amount they owed, or even claimed they had never borrowed the money in the first place. Some time in prison might 'persuade' them to settle their debts. But of course, that wouldn't work for people who just didn't have it. In those cases, friends and relatives might be encouraged to pay off at least some of the debt. This way they could get their loved one out of prison. And there were other possibilities ... once they were in prison, the debtor could ask for help from certain special charities. And rich gentlemen sometimes left money in their wills to help needy debtors.

The debtors' prison was very large — it could hold 500 people — and that's because it was quite common for a debtor's whole family to go into prison with them. It wasn't the law that the entire family had to go to prison, but often they had nowhere else to go – the debtor was usually a man, often married with children. If he lost everything, his poor family would have nowhere to live, and the only alternative was the workhouse, which was a terrible place – trust me, even worse than prison. Given a choice like that, many families decided to take their chances in gaol. In fact, here at Lancaster Castle, conditions for some debtors were so good that the place got the nickname 'Hansbrow's Hotel'. James Hansbrow took over my job, and was governor of the prison from 1833 until 1862. He must have been a good-natured man, for people used to send letters here addressed to 'Hansbrow's Hotel, Lancaster'.

Now most debtors' prisons had a Masters' Side and a Common Side. The Masters' Side was where wealthier debtors lived. These were people who might not have paid their debts, but still had access to money – either

Inside the first-class day room for debtors – looks nothing like prison!

their own, or some friend or relative's. There was a range of different cells available, and the debtors were charged rent depending on the size. So it *was* a bit like a hotel room ... though not always with a view. If they had enough money, debtors could even pay a poorer debtor to be their servant. Imagine that! Playing the gentleman even inside a prison cell. But there was more. Some debtors' prisons had shops, restaurants, barbers and tailors to cater for those staying on the Masters' Side. In those places, life wasn't too bad at all. Debtors drew up their own set of rules, such as no swearing and no preaching, to regulate the behaviour of their fellow prisoners. Anyone who broke the rules was fined. The money collected was saved up and spent on a yearly dinner. When there was a general election, the debtors held mock elections, with individuals representing either the Tories or the Whigs. These things were taken very seriously — speeches were given, and there were plenty of dirty tricks, with some candidates bribing other debtors to get more votes. Usually the winner was the one who told the best jokes! Things sometimes got very noisy and a bit out of hand, especially if wine or brandy had been smuggled in. More than once I had to send in the turnkeys to quieten things down. At Lancaster Castle, the Masters' Side was the new wing built between 1794 and 1796.

But things were very different on the Common Side. At Lancaster Castle, this was in the gatehouse, and it was where penniless debtors were kept. Conditions were very bad, with people sometimes forced to share

Some of the characters incarcerated for not paying their way

a bed with two or even three other people. They were given a small allowance of food, but this was often not enough, and prison reports mention some debtors who were so hungry, they were too weak to get out of bed. Those who had a skill (like weaving) could earn a bit of extra money by making things to sell on the outside, and special workshops were provided for this purpose. Many, however, were forced to rely on the charity of others. They faced a very uncertain future – unsure if they would ever get out of prison.

The 1869 Bankruptcy Act changed the law regarding debt, and from that point onwards, debtors' prisons gradually became a thing of the past. Once it had gone out of use, the debtor's wing at Lancaster Castle was used to hold male prisoners. No more parties!

Up close to the panopticon

The Female Penitentiary

BY 1818, THINGS WERE CHANGING. More and more people were being sent to prison, and that included women. But where was I supposed to put them? We simply did not have enough cells in the Female Felons' Tower to cope. Ideally, we needed to build a new and bigger tower for them. The problem though, was that there was just no space left in the castle to build one. So a decision was made to pull down one of the medieval towers. It was known as the Dungeon Tower, and although we don't know exactly when it was built it was probably about 500 years old when it was demolished.

I remember at the time some people in the town were saying it was a shame to pull down something so old, but of course they didn't have to deal with the terrible conditions in there. The Dungeon Tower might have been suitable as a prison in medieval times — but not in the nineteenth century. Why, there was almost no light or ventilation in there, and in the mornings when we went to open up and go in, the smell was so bad that we had to open the door wide and stand back for at least fifteen minutes, until the worst of the stench had escaped. A lot of prisoners became very ill from being kept in the Dungeon Tower, and I was not sorry to see it go. Especially as it was going to be replaced by something as modern as the new Female Penitentiary. Talk about cutting edge!

The tower with the all-seeing view

You see, the design of this tower was based on a new idea by a man called Jeremy Bentham (1748–1832). He tried to solve the problem of how to watch over hundreds of prisoners when you only had a few turnkeys to stand guard. Today of course you have cameras. But we didn't – and it was almost impossible to know what was going on inside the prison most of the time. We couldn't be everywhere at once, could we? But Bentham came up with an idea that he called 'The Panopticon'. That's a Greek word meaning 'to see everything'. He thought it would be possible to see everything if the cells were just arranged differently.

Instead of having a long corridor of cells, the ones in this tower are arranged in a semi-circle and the idea was that if the turnkey stood in the centre, they would be able to see in all of the cells without moving – just by turning around. The cells did not have solid wooden doors in my day, they were just bars. So you really could see what was going on in all of the cells – it was a genius idea.

When the prison was being rebuilt, the layout was also designed like Bentham's panopticon. There was a central watchtower, called the Turnkeys' Lodge, and around this they constructed triangular prison yards. From up above, it looked a bit like a lady's fan. All the turnkeys had to do was turn around and they could see everything the prisoners were getting up to, without moving from the comfort of their lodge. If they saw anything suspicious, they could signal down to the turnkeys in the yards and they would go investigate. If you look at the plan below, you can see how it would have worked.

Sadly, though Bentham's idea was very good in some ways, it was very bad in others, and the panopticon prison had to be abandoned after only a short time. This kind of prison was very expensive to build, which might have been okay if it wasn't for the *other* problem. Fact is, the prisoners felt like they were being watched all the time, and that had a very bad effect on their mental health. Some were actually driven mad by this system, and that's why the building of panopticons was stopped. Today, this tower is one of the few surviving prison examples of Jeremy Bentham's panopticon idea. So just you watch your step while you're in Lancaster Castle – because I can see you!

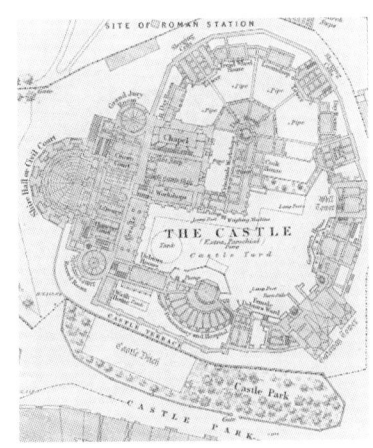

A castle plan, 1845

The dreaded crank

Prison Work

BEFORE I CAME TO THE CASTLE, most prisoners here did not have to do any work. Now I don't mean to brag, but I changed all that whilst I was governor. You see, John Howard believed that making prisoners do some form of work would help with prison order and discipline. He wanted to stop the chaos he had encountered in many prisons. Work would give prisoners something useful to do whilst they were here, and it would also raise money for the prison — we could sell what the prisoners made. Not only that, but if we gave the prisoners a share of the money, it meant they would not be penniless when they left us. And if they were not penniless, maybe they'd be less likely to go back to a life of crime — get it? They might even have learned something useful like a skill they could use to get a job on the outside.

At various times during the nineteenth century, prisoners at Lancaster Castle made and repaired shoes and clothes, made hammocks or wound wool. Female prisoners tended to clean the prison, work in the laundry or mend clothing and bedding.

Of course, some prisoners already had a skill when they came in. For example, by the early nineteenth century, Lancashire was a great textile-producing county and some of the prisoners were skilled weavers. So it

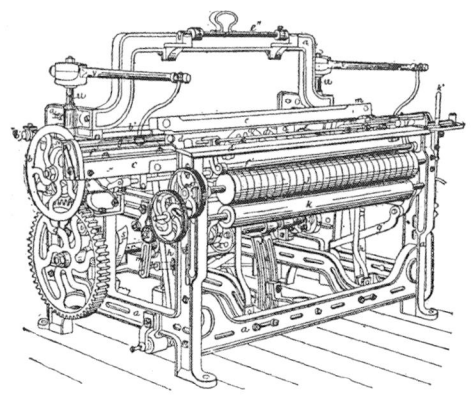

Why not weave to while away a stay?

made perfect sense for us to set up a weaving workshop with looms, so the weavers could produce cloth. We even managed to get a power supply going, though it's probably not what you're thinking ...

By the 1820s, something called a treadwheel was being introduced into many prisons as another form of work. The treadwheel was a huge wooden wheel with steps fitted to the outside of it, and all along this wheel were compartments big enough for a man to stand in (take a look at the illustration on the next page). The prisoners would put a foot onto a step and then on to the next one as they made the wheel go around — it was like climbing an endless flight of stairs, and very tiring. Prisoners would take turns with it — they'd be on the treadwheel for fifteen minutes and then have a five-minute rest while someone else did the work. Then another fifteen minutes on and five minutes off, and so forth. We had two treadwheels at Lancaster Castle — one provided power, through a series of belts, to the looms used for weaving, whilst the power from the other wheel was used to raise water from a well. The prisoners climbed ninety-six steps a minute — that's more than one every second! And during the day a man could 'climb' more than 10,000 feet (3,000 metres). Just the thing if you're planning an expedition to Mount Everest ...

But I know what you are thinking — if you aren't, what good is that? Well working the treadwheel wouldn't

A sketch of the treadmill in action

have taught them much of a skill, I reckon you're right about that. At best, it improved prisoners' fitness. But things like the treadwheel started to be used more and more when attitudes towards prisons started to change yet again. John Howard thought prison should help rehabilitate prisoners, help turn them away from crime so that they could become useful members of society when released. But by the 1840s, that kind of thinking was out of fashion. Work like the treadwheel was originally just a way of creating power for other things, but it became the preferred kind of work. Most treadwheels in other prisons didn't even create any power – the prisoners climbed for no reason, just to wear them out. This was the same time when the silent system (which we talked about before) was introduced into prisons. You see, work that involved too much thinking was no good – people wanted prisoners to spend all their time thinking about their bad behaviour and all that.

So mindless tasks were the order of the day. The treadwheel was one, but there was also something called the crank. The crank was just a handle that turned – a bit like the handle on a music box, only bigger as you had to put both hands on it to make it turn. There was also a counter on it, and every time you turned the handle the counter went up by one. Yep – that's all there was to it. No power was created – prisoners just turned the handle for the sake of turning the handle. As you can imagine, it was mind-numbingly boring. Prisoners would sometimes do this 'work' in their cell, or in a special room, and the turnkey would order them to do a certain number of turns before breakfast, lunch, and dinner. But the tricky bit was, each crank was adjustable. You could make the handle more, or less, difficult to turn. If the prisoner had been well behaved, then the turnkey would usually make it easier to turn – that way the work was quicker to do. If the prisoner was a bad one, though – well, they would have to work a lot harder and a lot longer before they got anything to eat.

Another form of mindless labour (used from 1862) was oakum picking, and this was probably the most hated job in prison. Each prisoner would be given a length of rope – about a foot (30cm) long – and a small hook. The rope had been used on sailing ships and come to the end of its useful life, and the prisoners had to unpick it. First, though, they had to break off a layer of tar that had protected

Oakum: humdrum

Oakum picking left your fingers raw and bleeding

it whilst at sea. Then they used the hook to separate out the individual strands that made up the rope. Oh, it was terrible work! They were hunched up all day, which made their back and shoulders ache, their fingers would get cut and bleed from dealing with the tar and rope, and worst of all this work created a lot of dust which got onto the chest and gave them coughs and lung diseases.

Thankfully, ideas changed once again. The silent system came to an end by the beginning of the twentieth century, and the work available in modern prisons is much better. Now, work is more varied and is designed to form part of the prisoners' rehabilitation – just what John Howard wanted all along. It includes things like working in the kitchens, gardening, computer skills, cobbling, carpentry, furniture making, tailoring and taking educational courses. All of these provide prisoners with skills and qualifications which can help them find a job when the day comes for their release. Beats turning a handle, doesn't it?

Annual General Session, Preston, September 7th, 1826.

DIETARY.

I.

For Prisoners sentenced to hard labour, for convicted Prisoners not sentenced to hard labour, but ordered by the Visiting Justices to be set to work, and for Prisoners before Trial who do not maintain themselves, but who work.—

MALES AND FEMALES.

20 ounces of household Bread, daily, served out in three portions, at Breakfast, Dinner and Supper.

4½ ounces of Oatmeal, daily, made into two quarts of Pottage, and served out, one quart for Breakfast and one quart for Supper, daily.

3½ ounces of Salt, weekly.

DINNERS—Sundays and Wednesdays } 1lb. of Beef, boiled, and 1lb. of Potatoes, each day, with liberty for the Visiting Justices to substitute an equivalent of Herrings for Beef.

Mondays and Thursdays } 1 gill of Peas boiled in the Broth and Bones from the last boiling of Beef, made into one quart of Soup each day, with the like liberty to substitute equivalent of Rice for Peas.

Tuesdays and Fridays 1½lbs. of Potatoes each day.

Saturdays .... 1 quart of Stew, made from Cowheads, in the proportion of five Cowheads to one hundred Prisoners, and with liberty for the Visiting Justices to make such alterations, (if any) as they may find necessary.

2.

For Prisoners before Trial who do not maintain themselves, and who do not work, and for all other Prisoners, (except such as are sick) who cannot maintain themselves, and who do not work.—

MALES AND FEMALES.

20 ounces of household Bread, daily, served out in three portions, at Breakfast, Dinner and Supper.

4½ ounces of Oatmeal, daily, made into two quarts of Pottage, and served out, one quart for Breakfast and one quart for Supper, daily.

4½ ounces of Salt, weekly.

10lbs. of Potatoes, weekly.

And all such articles of Food and Provisions for criminal Prisoners shall be cooked in the regular cooking houses within the Prison, and not by the Prisoners individually.

Prison Food

SO IF THE PRISONERS had to do all that work, what did we feed them on? Well, I'll tell you. They had a certain food allowance every week – in 1836, prisoners were provided with the following:

> 7lb (3.2kg) of bread
> 2.5lb (1.1kg) of oatmeal (made into a kind of porridge)
> 10lb (4.5kg) of potatoes
> 1.5lb (680g) of beef
> 5oz (141g) of rice
> 1.5 gills (214ml) of peas
> 4oz (113g) cheese

Now those metric figures are approximate, but you'll have to bear with me – we used the good old Imperial weights and measures in my day ... Anyway, the oatmeal was for breakfast, and most of the bread was used for lunches, but for dinner we made a hot meal every day. Want to know the menu? Well, to the best of my recollection, it was a kind of pattern.

On Mondays, they got half a pound (226g) of boiled beef with potatoes.

Tuesdays, it was one quart (1.14 litres) of rice soup – that had potatoes too.

Wednesdays, it would be half a pound of boiled beef and potatoes.

Thursdays, they got one quart of pea soup with more potatoes.

Fridays, probably half a pound of boiled beef made into scouse (that's a kind of stew with potatoes).

Saturdays, it was potatoes ... and cheese.

But Sundays were special – then they had one quart of stew made from cow shins. The proportion was one shin to every fourteen prisoners.

Not bad, eh? Are you getting hungry? Well *you* might not like the sound of cow shin, but in fact, in an 1840 report on the prison, many of the castle's prisoners said they thought they were a lot better off inside than outside. They certainly thought they were better fed! These kinds of comments were echoed by other prisoners in other prisons, and they do make it seem like prison was not really that bad. But then, what else were they going to say? That the

place was terrible and the staff were monsters? Prisoners knew if they said things like that, they would be talking about governors like me and turnkeys like my boys, and when the report was produced, well those people were not going to be too
pleased. You can't blame them for worrying that if they said anything bad, and the governor got to hear about it, they would be in trouble and be punished.

So many prisoners probably made things sound better than they were. And yet it was comments like these that were picked up and unfortunately misunderstood by some very influential people at the time. This led them to think that prison was not bad enough – not enough of a punishment – so they wrote to the government to complain. They demanded that things be tightened up in prisons, and for a time they got their way. They insisted that prison should be 'hard labour, hard food and hard beds'. That's why the silent system was introduced, as well as all those horribly boring forms of work we talked about earlier. And yes, they also made sure the beds were as hard and uncomfortable as possible.

These people did not believe in rehabilitation. They just wanted prisoners to feel punished. Well we tried it that way for a while, but as I said before, as an experiment it was a complete failure. This kind of treatment was soon abandoned – but not before it made a lot of prisoners' lives very miserable indeed.

We have a nice line of halberds upstairs

Hadrian's Tower

NOW THIS TOWER IS VERY OLD — it was built by King John in 1210. Most people seem to consider that King John was a pretty bad king, and you may have come across him in some of the stories about Robin Hood. But here at the castle, we have a bit of a soft spot for him because he liked the north of England, and he particularly liked Lancaster. He granted the town its very first market charter, and he spent a huge amount of money on this castle — £540. Now that may not *sound* like a lot of money, but today that would be worth about £500,000, and that was enough to build a gatehouse at the front of the castle, and two round towers with a connecting wall between them at the back — all constructed in stone! This was one of the round towers.

So you may be wondering if it was built by King John, why is it called Hadrian's Tower? Blame it on the Victorians — they thought it had been built by the Romans, and so they named it after the emperor who built the great Roman wall a little further north — Hadrian. We now know the Romans had nothing to do with the tower, but still the name stuck. I suppose it should really be called John's Tower, but I guess that wouldn't be very popular.

Restraining chairs beckon

When it was built, the tower would have been used for defence, and at the time it was very modern and technologically advanced. Do you remember when we were talking about the Keep, and how I told you anyone attacking the castle could try and make it fall down by digging a tunnel to one of the corners? Well, a round tower has no corners, so you can't do that – problem solved! It would have had two floors originally, and a flat roof, and you can still see the arrow slits where archers would stand, firing arrows at anyone attacking the castle. They are blocked up now, but you can still have a look.

Today, this tower is full of some of the things they used in my day to punish people who broke the law. There's a scold's bridle, which was used on women who gossiped too much, told lies about their neighbours and so forth, or got caught fighting in the street – troublemakers, in other words. It's a horrible thing – went over their head and had a metal bar in it that went down over their tongue, so they couldn't speak. They would then be taken into town on a market day with a sign around their necks labelling them and telling the whole world about their crimes. People used to call them names, make fun of them ... well they couldn't answer back, could they? Or they'd throw things like rotten fruit and vegetables at them. There's also the cat-o'-nine-tails and the birch rod. The cat was a fearsome thing used on adult men who broke the rules in the prison. They would be whipped across the back with it as a punishment. The birch was used on younger folk – the under 15s – for the same reason, only this was used on the hands. I guess they felt a *little* sorry for the younger ones ...

You can also see two restraining chairs and a set of leather straps.

Manacles on display – can you see how they would be worn?

These were for what we called 'lunatics' – people with mental illness. Sometimes these people ended up in the prison not because they'd done anything wrong, but just because there was no local hospital to take them.

They needed to be kept somewhere secure, so the castle seemed a good option. Well, I didn't think it was right – I told the government they shouldn't be here – but until a hospital was built, there was no other treatment than restraint. We just had to do our best, but I have to admit, tying people to chairs wasn't very good.

Watch your tongue!

Transportation to the Colonies

Around the walls of Hadrian's Tower, you can see lots of different examples of handcuffs and leg irons that were used to restrain prisoners. There is a very long set that goes right the way around the wall, with large iron hoops on it. This was used on people who had been found guilty of very serious crimes, like forgery (making false money), and had been sentenced to 'Transportation to the Colonies'. After 1788 this meant that they would be sent to Australia for the length of their sentence – that could be seven years, fourteen years, or even the rest of their life.

Not that it mattered really, because even if you only got seven years the government did not bring you back home afterwards – you had to make your own way back. Australia is on the other side of the world and back then it would have cost an absolute fortune to get back – you might as well have been left on the moon. Most people never came back at all – they simply started new lives in Australia once they were set free.

The long chain was used when the convicts who were going to be transported were being taken to the ships, which left from the south coast – places like Plymouth,

Chatham or Portsmouth. The prisoners would be chained in a long line, one behind the other, and the hoops went around their necks. They also wore ankle chains and handcuffs, and from Lancaster they had to walk about 300 miles to the docks like that! Can you imagine it? I sometimes went along with them, together with some of the turnkeys as guards, and it usually took us about six weeks to walk all that way. Not that I actually walked – I had a horse, but even so I was glad when it was over. For the prisoners, though, that was just the beginning; they then had the whole long voyage to Australia to do, and that took anywhere between six and ten months. And then once they landed, they had to do hard labour for the term of their sentence.

   I still remember taking a couple of children down to those docks back in 1788 – George and Elizabeth Youngson they were called. They came from Lancaster,

Can you imagine walking from Lancaster to Plymouth wearing a set of these?

Convict ship *Neptune*

and had been caught stealing money from a warehouse. At the time of their crime, two years earlier, Elizabeth was thirteen years old and her little brother George was twelve. Just kids you'd say today, but they only just escaped the death penalty. Maybe one day I'll write another book and tell you all about them ... but in the meantime, there's something to think about next time you get into trouble and get told off ...

The inside of one of the Old Cells: from ponies to prisoners to powder for pistols

The Old Cells

WHEN I FIRST ARRIVED HERE, this area was a stable block full of horses, but John Howard, the prison reformer I told you about, thought the space could be better used to provide some additional cells – so that's what we did. We converted it into extra cells, which were ultra modern in their day. You see, John Howard believed prisoners should be kept separate from one another at night, rather than in big dormitories. He worried chattering away with each other was a bad influence – and prisoners might just learn how to be a better criminal and not get caught next time! So these cells are built along his guidelines. They are big enough for one person, with space for a bed at the back of the cell. There would also have been a bucket, which was the toilet, and sometimes a chair. Of course sometimes we were too crowded to have only one person to a cell, and we would have to put another prisoner in. That's why there are two hooks in the walls – you could sling a hammock between them for the extra prisoner to sleep on. The doors were made out of some old wood that was just lying around. It was from trees cut down in the 1500s – well, did you think you invented recycling?

John Howard was also keen to clean up prisons and make them more hygienic so that fewer people died from disease. That why each cell has a vent above the door to let fresh air in. Back in my day, we didn't know that much about disease, and we thought it was caused by breathing in 'bad air' — and you knew it was bad because of the terrible smell! Doctors said we had to let more air in, and get it circulating, so that is what we were trying to do. It may not have cut down disease as much as we would have liked, but it certainly made the place smell better, so it wasn't a bad thing after all.

The area outside the cells was the dayroom, where the prisoners would spend their time between finishing work and being locked up for the night. There is a fireplace, and also a window which is now blocked up, but used to look out onto the courtyard. This could be opened to let in even more fresh air.

You can see the air vents above each cell door

Hammocks could be slung from the walls

These cells were used for a variety of prisoners. At one time they were used for debtors, then they were used for prisoners who were waiting for their trial, and finally in the early twentieth century, they were used as special punishment cells. These were for prisoners who had broken the rules and had to spend a few days on their own.

During the Napoleonic Wars (1793–1815), though, they had a very different use. We had some soldiers stationed here, and they needed somewhere to store their gunpowder. I have to say that having so much gunpowder around the place made me very nervous! That's why the floors are stone in the dayroom, but wood in the cells. The wooden floors were put in to reduce the chance of sparks being produced by the nails in the soldiers' boots. Or if something was accidentally dropped whilst we had gunpowder in there – well, we were trying to keep the whole castle from blowing sky high.

The Shire Hall

NOW THIS IS A ROOM! In fact, it's one of the most spectacular rooms in the whole north of England. It was built in 1798 and was designed by a man called Thomas Harrison, who came from Chester. It's a marvel of engineering because it's actually built on top of part of the old moat that used to run around the castle, so the ground underneath is quite soft. To get around this problem, Harrison had to hammer huge tree trunks into the ground so that the foundations could sit on something solid and stable. Imagine that — this whole thing is resting on wood!

The room is very grand because it was used as the 'civil court' — the place where people could bring arguments they were having which they could not settle. For example, if two people were arguing over who owned a particular piece of land, and each refused to back down, then they could bring their argument here and let the court decide. Back in my day, only the very rich were able to do this as they were the only ones who could afford to hire lawyers — it was very expensive to pay someone to argue for you. That's why this courtroom looks so grand — it's where rich people argued over money or possessions, so it had to look the part.

The canopy is made of Coade Stone, a material invented by Eleanor Coade, a baked mixture of clay and glass

Back then, when there was no television or internet, watching the trials in court was one of the great forms of entertainment, and people used to cram in to watch. It's said that up to 2,000 people sometimes stood in

Up to 2000 people squeezed in to watch a trial? Hands, face, no space!

here to listen to the arguments – talk about packed in like sardines! It's a wonder they didn't all faint. If you look closely at the photographs you can see where everyone sat. There were special seats that were saved for the judges' friends and family, and some set aside for rich ladies. The furniture was all made by Gillows of Lancaster, and the three portraits that you can see are of gentlemen who represented Lancaster in parliament during the eighteenth and nineteenth centuries. The magnificent canopy over the judge's bench is made from Coade stone, which is moulded like plaster but is much harder.

On the back wall are over 600 shields. The large ones along the top belong to all the kings and queens from Richard I (1189–1199) to Charles III (2022–present). The middle-sized ones along the bottom are of the constables of Lancaster Castle; these are the people

The largest public display of heraldry in the country

Ornate plasterwork depicting the Red Rose of Lancashire

who used to be in charge of looking after the castle, and defending it if it was attacked. The smaller ones are of the high sheriffs of Lancashire, who were responsible for keeping law and order in the county, and collecting all the taxes for the government.

Some of the designs are real works of art, and they can tell us a lot about the person who had them made. We call the designs 'coats of arms', and sometimes there are visual clues about things like the person's job, their interests or where they came from. Others make clever jokes on their name; for example, the Standish family coat of arms has three standing dishes – get it? And Alexander Fordyce has ... *four dice*! You can see some more examples in the photographs. Now you might be

wondering why some of the shields are just plain green. Well, sometimes those shields are for people we know held a particular office in a particular year, but their coat of arms has been lost over time – we just don't know what it is supposed to look like, so we left it plain. But *some* are for people who did something bad later in their lives, and were stripped of their right to have a coat of arms by the king or queen. There are always a few bad apples, so their blank shield is for disgrace. And one is for a person who belonged to the Religious Society of Friends, known as the Quakers. Quakers like things to be plain! So he would not have wanted a fancy coat of arms. So you see, every picture – or at least every shield – does tell a story ...

Use this spare shield to design your own coat of arms – maybe one day we'll see it in the Shire Hall!

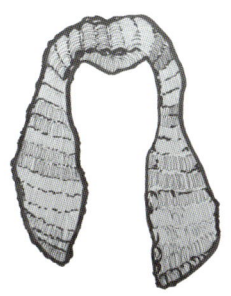

The Library

THE LIBRARY IN LANCASTER CASTLE doesn't have any exciting stories or magical adventure books. This is where we keep the books which lawyers might need to consult during a trial. There are more next door in the Barristers' Robing Room, which is a small room where the lawyers put on their wigs and gowns before going into court. You have to look the part, you know.

But speaking of looking the part, it doesn't look like it now, but when I first came here in the 1780s this room was called the Crown Hall, and this is where criminal trials took place until 1795, when the new Crown Court was built. When it stopped being used for trials, this room was remodelled by Thomas Harrison for its present use. The magnificent ceiling he put in looks like wood – but Ha! Fooled you! It isn't wood at all, it's plaster painted to look like wood. This kind of work is called *trompe l'oeil* – a fancy French phrase for

Real wood? Fake news!

fancy painting that 'tricks the eye'. It was very popular at the time. Hardly anyone can tell it isn't really wood.

The original Crown Hall was constructed on the orders of King John in about 1210, and was used for trials for almost 600 years. Some of our most well-known cases were heard in this room, and these include our two most infamous ones as follows.

The Lancashire Martyrs: These were the trials of fifteen Catholic men who were accused of High Treason (crimes against the state) between 1584 and 1646. This was when, as a Protestant country, the government and the Church of England considered Catholics disloyal. They were viewed with a great deal of

The skull of martyr, Ambrose Barlow.

suspicion – in fact, it was illegal even to be a Catholic priest in England at that time. In the vast majority of cases, Catholics were completely loyal to the king or queen. But that didn't stop the government persecuting many of them. All fifteen of the Catholic Martyrs were found guilty and executed. Those who were not priests (but had helped to hide them) were hanged. But the priests were hanged, drawn and quartered – an even more terrible death which was designed to discourage others from becoming Catholic priests and holding Mass.

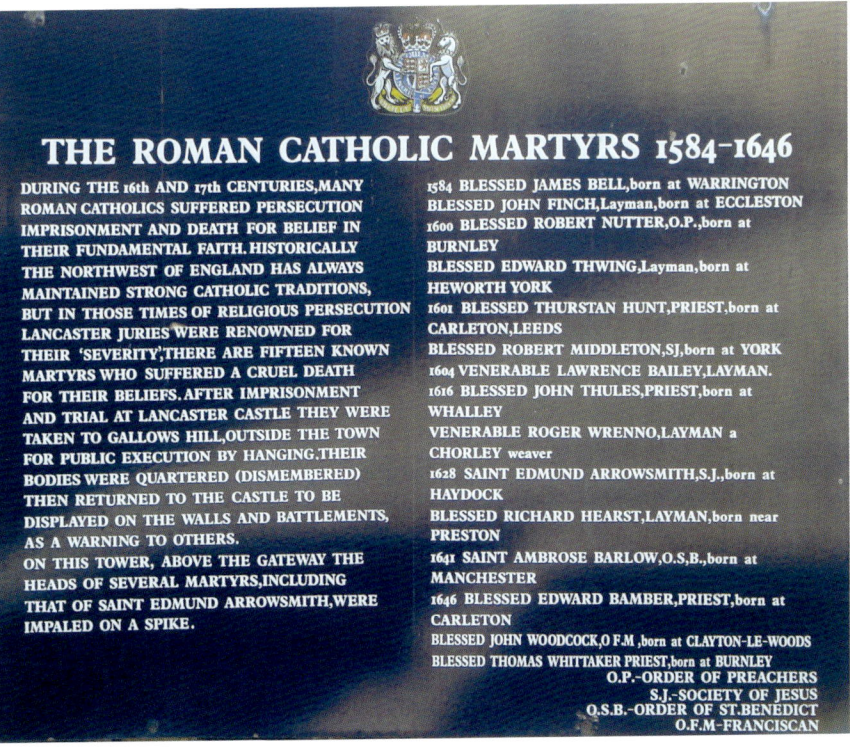

The mummified hand of Edmund Arrowsmith.

THE ROMAN CATHOLIC MARTYRS 1584-1646

DURING THE 16th AND 17th CENTURIES, MANY ROMAN CATHOLICS SUFFERED PERSECUTION IMPRISONMENT AND DEATH FOR BELIEF IN THEIR FUNDAMENTAL FAITH. HISTORICALLY THE NORTHWEST OF ENGLAND HAS ALWAYS MAINTAINED STRONG CATHOLIC TRADITIONS, BUT IN THOSE TIMES OF RELIGIOUS PERSECUTION LANCASTER JURIES WERE RENOWNED FOR THEIR 'SEVERITY'. THERE ARE FIFTEEN KNOWN MARTYRS WHO SUFFERED A CRUEL DEATH FOR THEIR BELIEFS. AFTER IMPRISONMENT AND TRIAL AT LANCASTER CASTLE THEY WERE TAKEN TO GALLOWS HILL, OUTSIDE THE TOWN FOR PUBLIC EXECUTION BY HANGING. THEIR BODIES WERE QUARTERED (DISMEMBERED) THEN RETURNED TO THE CASTLE TO BE DISPLAYED ON THE WALLS AND BATTLEMENTS, AS A WARNING TO OTHERS.
ON THIS TOWER, ABOVE THE GATEWAY THE HEADS OF SEVERAL MARTYRS, INCLUDING THAT OF SAINT EDMUND ARROWSMITH, WERE IMPALED ON A SPIKE.

1584 BLESSED JAMES BELL, born at WARRINGTON
BLESSED JOHN FINCH, Layman, born at ECCLESTON
1600 BLESSED ROBERT NUTTER, O.P., born at BURNLEY
BLESSED EDWARD THWING, Layman, born at HEWORTH YORK
1601 BLESSED THURSTAN HUNT, PRIEST, born at CARLETON, LEEDS
BLESSED ROBERT MIDDLETON, SJ, born at YORK
1604 VENERABLE LAWRENCE BAILEY, LAYMAN.
1616 BLESSED JOHN THULES, PRIEST, born at WHALLEY
VENERABLE ROGER WRENNO, LAYMAN a CHORLEY weaver
1628 SAINT EDMUND ARROWSMITH, S.J., born at HAYDOCK
BLESSED RICHARD HEARST, LAYMAN, born near PRESTON
1641 SAINT AMBROSE BARLOW, O.S.B., born at MANCHESTER
1646 BLESSED EDWARD BAMBER, PRIEST, born at CARLETON
BLESSED JOHN WOODCOCK, O.F.M, born at CLAYTON-LE-WOODS
BLESSED THOMAS WHITTAKER PRIEST, born at BURNLEY
O.P.-ORDER OF PREACHERS
S.J.-SOCIETY OF JESUS
O.S.B.-ORDER OF ST.BENEDICT
O.F.M-FRANCISCAN

The Lancashire Witches: These trials all took place in August 1612, and they are the most famous ever heard at the castle. The Lancashire Witches were not just one group of people, but the most famous of them were the Pendle Witches. The story goes that a young girl called Alison Device was begging on a road near Colne when she saw a peddler called John Law. She asked him to give her some pins, but he refused — well, she didn't have any money — and it was at this point that she is said to have cursed him. He immediately fell down and became very ill. His symptoms were exactly the same as those in someone who today we'd describe as having a stroke — he became paralysed down one side of his body, and he could not speak. Four hundred years ago, though, they did not have this medical knowledge, and believed he must have been bewitched. This led to an investigation of Alison, her family, and others in the Pendle area, which resulted in nine

Pendle Witches
Chattox and Redferne

A depiction of the hanging of the Pendle Witches

people being found guilty of witchcraft and hanged. Another woman, called Isobel Robey, who came from Windle, was also found guilty of witchcraft at the same time and hanged alongside those from Pendle.

Now I'll show you the new courtroom ...

The Hanging Court

The Crown Court

THIS COURTROOM WAS BUILT IN 1795, and became known as 'The Hanging Court' because between 1795 and 1835 more people were sentenced to death here than in any other courtroom in Britain except for the Old Bailey in London. Now it wasn't that the judges were more bloodthirsty or horrible than anywhere else — well I don't think so anyway — but at that time this court took in cases from a huge area — from Barrow to Warrington, which included Manchester and Liverpool. That meant many more cases were heard here than in other places, except London. So in terms of the *proportion* of people sentenced to death, it was probably no worse, or no better, than the rest of the country.

Today, trials can take place on any weekday. But when I was governor, the judges only came to Lancaster twice a year — in March and August. The sessions were known as 'the Assizes', which comes from a French word meaning 'to sit'. Even today court sessions are known as 'sittings'.

The Crown Court is very different from the Shire Hall, though — it's got an atmosphere. It's certainly not as grand and it is very dark and gloomy by comparison. If you look at the photograph opposite, you can see where all the different people stood or sat. There is a huge

79

painting of George III, who was the king when this room was built. The woodwork is all made by Gillows of Lancaster.

Inside the box where the defendant sits, known as 'the dock', we still have our branding iron and clamp. Until 1811, a judge could not only decide to send a convicted criminal to prison or Australia – he could also have him or her branded. This would happen right there in the dock. The criminal's left hand would be placed in the clamp, the branding iron would be heated up to red-hot and pressed into the hand just below the thumb – OUCH! They were branded with a letter M for *Malefactor,* which is a Latin word meaning 'evil-doer', and they would carry that mark for the rest of their lives. Anyone who saw it would know exactly what they had been up to.

And it wasn't always easy to cover it up. Just before giving evidence in a trial everyone had to swear an oath that they would tell the truth. You know, that's the part where they place their right hand on the Bible. But they also had to raise their *left* hand – and that was to show the court whether or not they already had a brand. If they had one, the whole court would know that they

Aha! A brand new hand

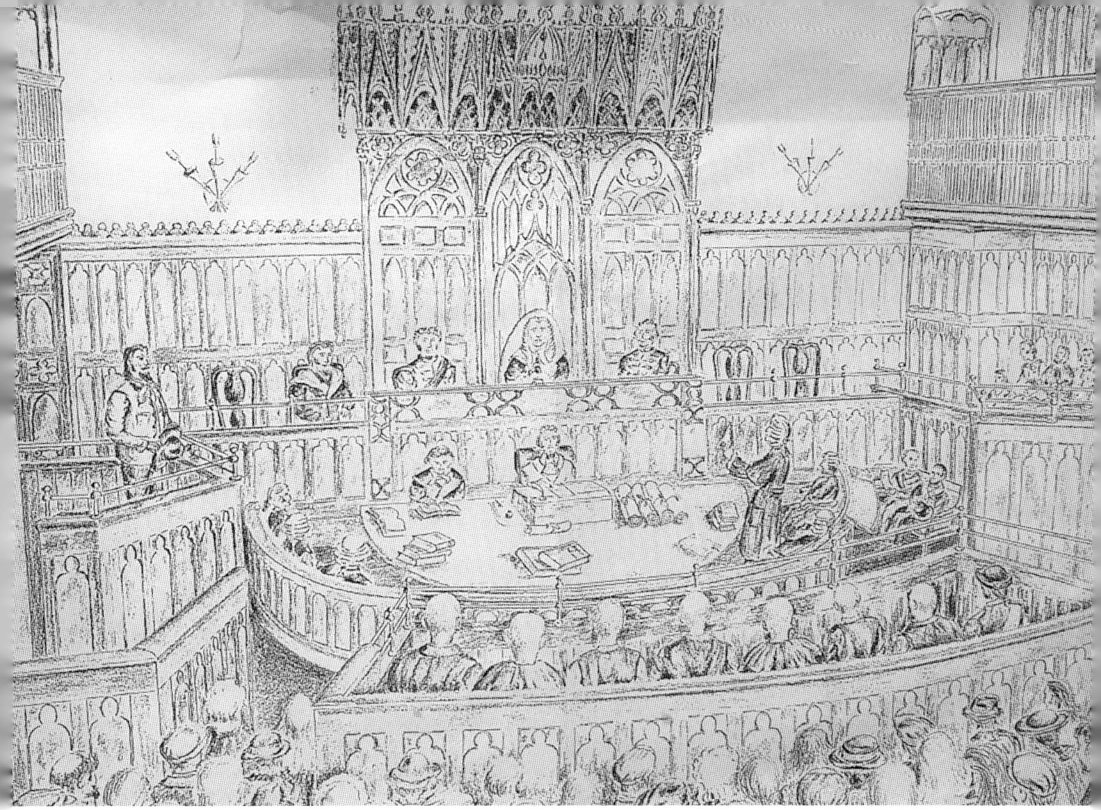

An illustration of the Crown Court in sitting

had been convicted of a crime, and so their word wasn't going to be worth much. Although no one has been branded since 1811, the tradition of raising the hand whilst taking the oath in court has remained in many countries to this day.

A
CALENDAR
OF THE
CROWN PRISONERS,
CONFINED
IN HIS MAJESTY'S GAOL,
THE
CASTLE OF LANCASTER,
The 4th Day of September, 1813.
William Farington Esquire, Sheriff.
Lancaster:
Printed by John Jackson, New Street.

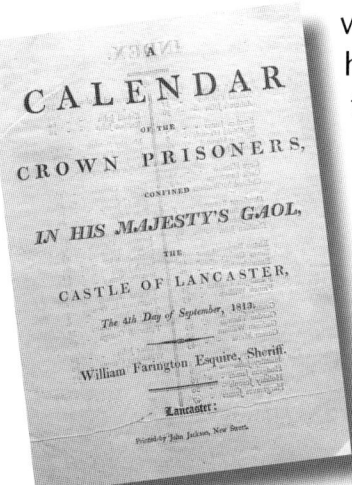

Trials could go on for quite a while, so you might be wondering how people managed to answer the call of nature. Well at the back of the jury box is a little door. They used to pass a pot through that for any member of the jury who wanted to go to the toilet during the trial! Thankfully, it's not used anymore – but I can still remember the smell!

A hangman's rope

The Drop Room

EVEN AFTER ALL THESE YEARS, this room still gives me the shivers. You see, when I was governor of the prison we had a punishment which the UK doesn't have any more – the death penalty – and between 1800 and 1865 it was in this room that those who were going to be hanged spent some of their final moments on Earth.

Until 1800 executions took place on Lancaster Moor, which is on a hill on the other side of town, roughly where Williamson's Park is now – that's where the Pendle Witches were hanged in 1612. But from 1800, the authorities decided that executions should be carried out at the castle, opposite the Priory Church, at a place which became known as 'Hanging Corner'. Over 200 people were executed at Hanging Corner.

Before coming into this room, the condemned spent some time in the prison chapel. They were then brought in through a connecting door. At exactly midday, the prison bell would toll and the door out onto the

A pinioning strap to stop the felons from fighting the hangman

Inside the Drop Room. See the execution bell by the door

scaffold would open, and they would be led outside. The scaffold was a large wooden platform which was built the day before the executions took place and taken down again the day afterwards.

Every time an execution was scheduled, about 8,000 people from all over Lancashire used to turn up to watch, and these included local schoolchildren who were brought along so they could see for themselves what happened to people who broke the law. So not your average school trip. Often the condemned person would give a speech from the scaffold, telling the story of how they came to commit their crime and encouraging others not to follow the same sorry path.

They would then be hanged, and afterwards they would be buried – either inside the castle walls or underneath what is now the car park at the back of the castle. I know – it sounds strange burying people like that when there's a church right next door. But you see, people who had been hanged were not usually allowed to be buried in a church cemetery.

The last person to be hanged at Hanging Corner was Stephen Burke in 1865. In 1868 the government put an end to public hangings, and after that, any executions took place inside the castle – usually in Chapel Yard. The last person to be hanged at Lancaster Castle was Thomas Rawcliffe in 1910.

The death penalty was abolished in the United Kingdom in 1965.

Right, let's move on …

Hanging Corner, outside the Drop Room, today

Queen Vic's ample throne

The Grand Jury Room

I ALMOST DECIDED TO SKIP THIS ROOM ... to be honest, I'm a bit old to be climbing all these stairs. But this room is worth seeing – not everyone knows what's inside.

Until the early 1930s this room was used by a group of men known as the 'Grand Jury'. Their job was to look at the evidence against a person accused of a crime and decide if there was enough of it for there to be a trial. So they would look at all the paperwork, and they would examine any witnesses there might be. These would stand in a special witness box while the Grand Jury questioned them. Having done all that and made their decision, the Grand Jury would then go into the Crown Court and sit in special gallery seats reserved for them. The leader would then hand a piece of paper over to the judge with their decision on it, and the defendant would either be tried in court or, if he was lucky, let go. The Grand Jury was abolished in the 1930s and replaced by the Crown Prosecution Service, which continues to decide whether trials should take place to this very day. They don't sit in the castle anymore though – they now have offices elsewhere.

Which is no bad thing, because now you can see it. The furniture in this room was all made by Gillows of Lancaster, and the chairs are

Inside the Grand Jury Room

absolutely unique. Each one has a head carved into the top of the backrest, and all of the heads are different. Some look like important men – judges perhaps, or even members of the Grand Jury – while others are of animals. Some are fantasy figures and look a little bit scary – take a look at the photographs to see some examples.

One head with a mane, one a ruff and one a collar – which is which?

There are also two judges' chairs in here, made in 1813. Originally one was meant for each of the courtrooms but they have now been retired from use.

You can also see a 'throne' which was made especially for Queen Victoria when she visited the castle in 1851. It was placed in the Shire Hall so that she could sit down whilst various people gave speeches welcoming her to Lancaster. You know how sometimes people can talk your ears off ... well just imagine if you have to stand there graciously nodding the whole time. Anyway, as it turned out, she managed to stand for the entire time, so she never actually sat in it. Still, it looks impressive – and it was made for her anyway, so close enough.

Oh, and one last thing – the ceiling looks like stone, but it's another tricky one – it's only painted plaster. A grand illusion for the Grand Jury room!

Painting rectangles on plaster – grandmaster art or a dead boring job for the most junior apprentice?

The Duke of Lancaster

NOW RIGHT AT THE BEGINNING of this little book, I mentioned who this castle belongs to. I hope you were paying attention, because now I'm going to ask you who it was ... you do remember, don't you? Yes, that's right – today, Lancaster Castle belongs to His Majesty King Charles III. But the reason it belongs to him is because he also has another title which might surprise you. He is the Duke of Lancaster.

Back in 1399, the 3rd Duke of Lancaster, Henry Bolingbroke, rebelled against King Richard II, who was a tyrant and a very bad king. Henry overthrew him and was made king himself. When he became King Henry IV, he should have given up his old title, Duke of Lancaster – I mean as king, why would he even need it? But there was a reason. You see, by 1399, the Dukes of Lancaster were the richest men in the whole country – richer even than the king. They held lands all over the country, and owned lots of other castles including Pontefract, Knaresborough, Bolingbroke and Tutbury. So to give up all that power and wealth wasn't easy – in fact, giving it to someone else would have been a very dangerous thing for Henry to do. After all, he had just overthrown the king, so what was to stop another Duke of Lancaster from doing the same thing to him? So he decided to keep it, and carry on being the Duke of Lancaster as well as being king. Henry's dukedom remained with the monarch, but separate to the crown – as his private possession. Talk about having your cake and eating it too!

Henry IV passed this system down to his heirs, and things have stayed that way ever since. Every king or queen since 1399 has also been the Duke of Lancaster and owned Lancaster Castle as a result. So even when Elizabeth II was Queen of England, she was the Duke of Lancaster rather than the Duchess. Why was this? Well more recently, it has just been tradition, but in the past there was good reason for it as well. It dates back to a time when female titles were viewed as lower than male titles. So back in the days of, say, Elizabeth I (1558–1603) it would not have been acceptable for the queen to take the title of duchess, because that would have made her lower status than all the dukes in the country – so they stuck with the male title. So there you are – that's why Her Majesty was the Duke of Lancaster when she was queen. Did you know that she was also the Duke of Normandy, as King Charles is now?

The lands belonging to a duke are known as a 'duchy', and so the lands of the Duke of Lancaster are known as the Duchy of Lancaster – and the castle is part of the Duchy. If you look at the flagpole on top of the gatehouse you can see that the flag flying there is of the Duke of Lancaster. Today, the main Duchy offices are in the Strand in London, but they also have offices right here in the castle.

In Lancashire when we drink a toast to His Majesty we always say: 'To the King, the Duke of Lancaster'. It's an odd way to say cheers, but that's history for you!

The Duchy of Lancaster owns several other castles. Have you been to any of them?

Knaresborough

Halton

Ogmore

Tutbury

Pickering

Peveril

Pontefract

Tickhill

Can you see any similarities with Lancaster Castle?

Bolingbroke

Lancaster Castle in the modern age

WELL I DON'T KNOW ABOUT YOU, but after hundreds of years' worth of stories, even a ghost will start to fade a little. But I always revive when we get to the twentieth century – because the castle went through a lot of changes then.

Lancaster Castle was still a prison right up until 1916, when suddenly everything changed. All of the prisoners were moved out to other prisons, and the reason for this was the First World War (1914–18). By 1916, lots of captured German soldiers were being sent to Britain as prisoners of war, and the government was finding it more and more difficult to find somewhere to put them. They needed to be kept safe and secure, so sometimes special prisoner of war camps were built. But the government also used places like this castle. You can see why they might have thought the walls – so thick and high – were ideal for the purpose. Even in my day, the castle was used for French POWs, but back then we just kept 'em in a different corner of the castle from everyone else. A hundred years later though, things

95

were done differently. They didn't think it was right to mix prisoners of war with criminals, so the criminal prisoners had to move out.

A German war grave at Cannock Chase

The castle was used to house prisoners of war until the end of the war, when all the German prisoners were sent home. Well, all except a few who died of Spanish Flu before they could be released. That was in 1919. Spanish Flu was a pandemic that affected the world between 1918 and 1920, and it killed millions of people. It's not really fair to call it Spanish Flu – no one really knows where it started. But it became big news when the King of Spain caught it, and so that's when most people heard about it and started calling it the Spanish Flu. The name just stuck! Sadly, three of our German prisoners of war caught the disease whilst in the castle and died.

After the war, the castle had a new purpose. It became a police training academy where new recruits, known as cadets, were trained. This was their home, where they trained, ate and slept. We had cops *and* robbers – just not at the same time!

Then came the Second World War (1939–45) and the castle was once again used for military purposes. The Royal Observer Corps was stationed here for a time. It

A Spitfire 'toppling' the smaller V-1 flying bomb by touching wingtips. The RAF knew where to find enemy aircraft because of information sent to them by the Royal Observer Corps

was their job to track enemy aircraft as they flew over the coast, usually on bombing raids. They'd mark their positions on maps, and send that information to the Royal Air Force, who would then send fighter planes, like Spitfires and Hurricanes, to stop them.

A pin badge (left) and cap badge of the Royal Observer Corps

The Observer Corps moved out part way through the war to other headquarters, and we also had a group called the Non-Combatant Corps stationed here. A non-combatant is someone who does not fight. These people are often called 'conscientious objectors'. This means someone who objects to fighting – they won't take part in it or even carry a gun - because of their conscience or religious beliefs. But that *doesn't* mean these people refused to help the war effort. Conscientious objectors often did other things to help, sometimes very dangerous work like helping the wounded on the battlefield, or defusing unexploded bombs that had fallen on cities like London. Here in Lancaster, they used to break down the

large food shipments arriving by train at the quay (next to the River Lune) into individual food parcels which were sent to soldiers on the frontline.

But after the war ended in 1945, the castle was pretty much unused – until the government decided to open it as a prison again in 1954. Well the walls were still just as thick I guess, so why not go back to the old business? And it remained a prison right up until the day the doors finally closed. That was 31 March 2011.

So now, here we are in the twenty-first century. I mean here *you* are. What do they call you these days? Tourists, that's right. I can tell you, we had none of you when I was governor here. Oh we might have had the occasional VIP (Very Important Person) like a visiting prince or lord, or sometimes a well-known foreign traveller or diplomat poke their nose in. But definitely no ordinary folk – at least, not the kind who could leave whenever they liked!

Tourists started coming in the late nineteenth century. Then for most of the twentieth century, the part of the castle where the courts sit was opened up – but only when trials were not taking place. Visitors were

allowed to see the courtrooms, Hadrian's Tower and the Old Cells. It became very popular, and we were one of the 'must see' places in the north of England. In the twenty-first century, they even started using the castle as a dramatic theatre setting – everything from plays by William Shakespeare to musical events. Then in 2012, the year of Queen Elizabeth II's Diamond Jubilee, they let the first visitors in over fifty years see the inside of the former prison on special tours held to celebrate. I guess it went well, because on 26 May 2013 the Duchy of Lancaster opened the castle to visitors permanently, and the rest is history. Which brings us right back to where we started – to the gatehouse where you came in. If you look around today, you'll probably see people gathering in the courtyard, waiting for the next tour. The guides may be only flesh and blood, but they know the stories of these walls almost as well as I do. At least, the ones that have happened so far ... but you never know what's around the corner.

You might think the twenty-first century is bang up-to-date, but there's still history being made here at the castle. For example, who can forget Covid-19? The pandemic had the whole country locked down and so the castle had to close too. Me and the other ghosts had the place to ourselves for months! Well it was us and the manager, Colin – he carried on looking after the place but he was all alone, poor man. Then in November 2021, Storm Arwen swept

The fallen Wych Elm outside the Priory

across Lancashire with winds up to one hundred miles an hour. Now these old walls have weathered many a storm, but Arwen gave us a right knock – in fact, a massive tree that was growing next door at the Priory toppled over, smashed through a stone wall, hit the castle, broke a lot of windows – including some in the Grand Jury Room – and even demolished part of an external staircase. To make matters even worse, it was the oldest tree in Lancaster! Now thankfully it happened at night, so no one was in the castle and no one got hurt – but the sight of that tree wedged against the walls with its roots in the air like it was no more than a matchstick – well, I never saw anything like that, and I've been around for hundreds of years! Then in 2022, sadly Queen Elizabeth passed away. Now that was the end of an era. She was succeeded by her son, and now King Charles is not only King, he's the new Duke of Lancaster too. So that means the castle has a new owner – guess you could say a new governor. It just goes to show, history never stops. It's all around us, and every one of us is part of it. A thousand years of history ... and counting.

Sunrise at Castle Hill… dawn of a new era?

Biography

WANT to know more about our narrator, John Higgin Jnr? We don't know all of the details of his life, but this much is certain.

JOHN Higgin Junior was born in 1764. His father, who was also called John Higgin, became governor of the prison at Lancaster Castle in 1776 and brought his family to live in the castle. He died seven years later at the age of 48, having caught gaol fever (typhus) from a prisoner who was already ill from the disease when he arrived at the castle. John Higgin Snr was considered a humane governor. He made a number of improvements to the prison, including drilling a hole through the wall of the Dungeon Tower to allow more fresh air into rooms which were otherwise dreadfully hot and smelly. Following his death, John Jnr (who was only 19 years old at the time!) was appointed governor and spent the next fifty years looking after the prison and its inmates.

LIKE his father, John Higgin Jnr was a humane man. In fact, he is often referred to as 'The Gentleman Gaoler'. He did his best, even under very difficult circumstances, to try and help prisoners. For example, he helped debtors complete the paperwork needed for their release, and he got his son, who was a Lancaster lawyer, to assist poor debtors without charging a fee. He is known to have given hungry prisoners food from his own house. He also wrote many letters to the government, urging them to build a suitable hospital in Lancaster to house people who were mentally ill rather than sending them to prison, where the conditions were unsuitable. A hospital was eventually built in 1816, thanks in part to his efforts. John Higgin Jnr also tried to improve the health of his prisoners through better sanitation and medical provision.

But not everyone approved. He did get into trouble in 1812, when a debtor wrote a letter to the government blaming him for the death of another prisoner. After a lengthy investigation, Higgin was found to be innocent of the charge. He did get told off though - for not keeping proper prison records!

There were some parts of his job that he found very difficult. As prison governor, John Higgin was expected to attend the hangings which took place at Lancaster Castle. He absolutely hated this, and the prison chaplain remarked that he was always very upset and distressed afterwards.

John Higgin resigned as governor in 1833, and was succeeded by James Hansbrow. Higgin left the castle but continued to live in Lancaster, in a house close to the cathedral. He died in 1847. You'll find a memorial tablet to him in Lancaster Priory Church, but his grave is now lost. Still, thanks to readers like you, he won't be forgotten – at least not as long as the castle stands. Now there's a memorial!

Timeline

AD 79
The Romans constructed a fort at Lancaster

AD 200–325
The fort enlarged and strengthened

AD 409
The Romans left Britain and abandoned the fort at Lancaster

1066
The Normans arrived in Britain

1093
Roger de Poitou, a Norman baron, founded Lancaster Castle. The castle keep dates from this time

1206
King John visited Lancaster Castle and subsequently spent a fortune on its development, including Hadrian's Tower, a gatehouse and the Crown Building

1265
The beginning of the Lancaster inheritance

1340
The Well Tower constructed around this time

1362
John O'Gaunt made the second Duke of Lancaster

1405
John O'Gaunt gateway built

1584–1646
Fifteen Catholics executed at Lancaster because of their faith

1597
Penal transportation began

1612
The Pendle Witches tried at Lancaster Castle and found guilty of witchcraft

1642
The English Civil War: Lancaster Castle taken by parliamentarians

c. 1653
The castle walls demolished as part of a country-wide demilitarisation

1660
Charles II restored and repairs to the castle began

1715
The first Jacobite Rebellion: nine rebels were hanged and their heads fixed on the gatehouse

1798
The Shire Hall built

1865
Stephen Burke was the last person to be publicly hanged at Lancaster Castle, for the murder of his wife

1869
The Bankruptcy Act brought the end of debtors' prisons

1914
The start of WWI and the closure of HMP Lancaster Castle

1916
Lancaster Castle became a German POW camp

1923
Lancashire County Council took the castle over from the Prison Commission and opened the County Police Academy

1929
LCC tried to buy the castle from the Prison Commissioners but the Duchy of Lancaster suddenly declared it was the true owner. The Duchy won the ensuing dispute but agreed to let the castle to LCC for 60 years

1937
The Police Academy closed

1939–1945
Royal Observer Corps and later Non-Combatant Corps were stationed at the castle

1957
Lancaster Castle back in use as a Category B Prison

1976
Regular tours of the castle began

1991
The Duchy Lease ended however an extension was granted to keep the prison open

2011
The last prisoners left HMP Lancaster Castle as it closed after 800 years of penal history

2022
Death of Queen Elizabeth, Duke of Lancaster, and accession of King Charles III

Glossary

BANKRUPTCY
when a person or business is unable to pay their debts

BRAND
a burn mark made on skin with a red-hot branding iron

BRANDING IRON
a long metal stick with a special design at the end to burn a mark onto a person or animal's skin

CAT O'NINE TAILS
a whip, split at one end into nine knotted cords

COADE STONE
a baked mixture of clay and glass, invented by Eleanor Coade

COMMON SIDE
the part of the debtors' jail where absolutely penniless debtors were sent

CONSCIENTIOUS OBJECTOR
a person who refuses to perform military service because of religious or moral stance

CRANK
a weighted handle for prisoners to turn for punishment

CROWN COURT
a court that deals with the most serious criminal offences

DEATH PENALTY
the punishment given out for the worst crimes, usually to be hanged around the neck until the offender had died

DEBTOR
a person who owes money to another

DUCHY
The land and other assets belonging to a dukedom

A courtyard view on a sunny day

FELON
a person who has committed a crime

FORTIFIED
made strong and capable of defending against attack

GATEHOUSE
a room over a gate, often used as a prison

GOVERNOR
the person in charge of a prison

GRAND JURY
the group of people who decided whether a trial should take place

HERALDRY
the shapes, colours, animals and other symbols used to create a coat of arms to represent a person or family, originally used by knights on their shields

INTEREST
the cost you charge to lend someone some money, or the extra price you have to pay if you borrow some

KEEP
a fortified tower within a castle, the last resort if the rest of the castle fell to enemies

KING'S EVIDENCE
when an accused person gives evidence against someone else in their gang, in the hope of being set free without trial, or a reduced sentence if convicted

LOOM
a mechanical device used to weave cloth

MALEFACTOR
a wrong-doer

MASTERS' SIDE
the part of a debtors' jail where wealthy people were sent. These were often people who would not, rather than could not, pay their debts

MARTYR
a person who is killed because of their religious beliefs

MURDER HOLES
holes built into a castle's defence through which boiling oil or tar could be poured onto attackers

NOOSE
a looped and knotted rope used to hang a felon

OAKUM
a loose fibre gleaned from untwisting and unpicking old rope

PANOPTICON
a prison with a central observation tower so the guard can see all the prisoners at any time

PENITENTIARY
a prison

PENTONVILLE STYLE
a style of prison named after the Pentonville Model Prison (1842) which introduced the silent and segregated system

PORTCULLIS
a heavy iron grating which can be lowered very quickly to shut off a castle gateway

PRISONER OF WAR
an enemy soldier held captive by opposing forces during a time of war

SILENT SYSTEM
the system in some prisons where inmates were not permitted to speak to one another

SCOLD'S BRIDLE
an iron frame worn over the head with a metal bit for the mouth, designed to humiliate and punish a woman

TAKING THE OATH
a promise taken before a person gives evidence in court that they will speak the truth

TRANSPORTATION
the act of sending convicted criminals, by sea, from Britain to America, the West Indies or Australia. This was ended in 1868

TREADWHEEL
a form of hard labour for prisoners operated by pushing a large wheel round with steps set into the shaft

TRIAL
the process where it is decided if a person is innocent or guilty of a crime

TROMPE L'OEIL
a fake wood effect painted upon plaster

TURNKEY
the person who locked prisoners away into their cells

Punishment

Punishments at Lancaster were dished out left, right and centre ... here are some more details about some of the penalties prisoners had to endure.

Shot drill

Shot drill included carrying a 26lb cannonball up and down the courtyard, putting it down and picking it up at the end of each leg. That's roughly how much a toddler weighs ...

Oakum picking

Oakum-picking was a task hated by many prisoners as it was monotonous, painful and labour-intensive. It was also a form of recycling; the worn-out rigging from sailing ships was cut into small pieces (about 2 feet each) and sent to county gaols (and workhouses) throughout the country to be 'picked'. Prisoners spent hours carefully separating all of the individual strands of hemp that comprised the rope by rubbing it on their legs and teasing it apart using a small hook and their fingers. Before they could begin this process, they also had to pick off a layer of tar which had been applied to the rope in order to protect it from the worst effects of the elements whilst at sea. The rooms in which this work was done were filled with dust; prisoners' legs and fingers would be blistered, and their backs and shoulders would ache due to their spending hours hunched over their work. Once separated out, the hemp would then be sent back to the shipyards to be remixed with tar and used as caulking (waterproofing) on the inside of new vessels.

The crank

The crank was also extremely unpopular with prisoners. At first sight, the crank looked fairly harmless: it consisted of a pedestal on the top of which was a wooden box with a handle on the side and a counter which registered how many times the handle had been turned. Prisoners would then be set a target to reach by a specified time, for example, so many turns before breakfast, before lunch, etc. The average for an adult prisoner was about 1800 per hour, for a juvenile about 1500. What made the crank particularly unpopular, however, was the fact that the tension of the handle could be set by a prison officer. Hence, a prisoner who had been well-behaved the previous day could have the tension set to its lowest point, allowing the handle to turn rapidly and easily. A prisoner who had misbehaved, however, could very well find themselves having to use both hands, and a considerable amount of effort, simply to turn the handle once. Cranks were usually placed by the wall of a room which had been provided with a small opening so that a prison officer could see the counter from a corridor and keep a check on the progress of the 'work'. These counters could be reset by turning a small screw, and this is the reason why prison officers were sometimes referred to as 'screws'.

The treadwheel

The first treadwheel at Lancaster Castle was installed in 1821. Another wheel was added later – the first treadwheel-powered machinery – and required 13 prisoners at a time (powering 23 pairs of power looms for weaving calico), whilst the other treadwheel pumped water from a well and required 12 prisoners at a time. Like most other treadwheels, those at Lancaster Castle had wooden partitions along them to prevent prisoners talking to each other.

From May to October they would walk the treadwheel for ten hours per day, doing 96 steps per minute and climbing 10,400 feet each day; they were allowed a five-minute rest for every 15 minutes of climbing. Females and prisoners under the age of 14 were exempt from this form of hard labour. Treadwheels were finally abolished by the 1898 Prison Act.

Police academy punishments

Police recruits weren't exempt from punishment when the academy was based at the castle. Recruits' misdemeanours were chastised with peeling potatoes, using small hooks to pick grass out of the cobbles outside the gatehouse, and polishing the cannonballs of the old cannon in the courtyard.

Image credits

iii: Medieval knight, Shutterstock
iv: The Witches' Tower dungeon steps, used by kind permission of the Duchy of Lancaster
v: James I of England, Shutterstock
vi–vii: An aerial view of Lancaster Castle, copyright Andrew Brier
viii: The Gatehouse, photograph by Colin Penny, used by kind permission of the Duchy of Lancaster
p.1: Higgin portrait, James Sant RA, private collection
p.1: Ragged hole effect, Shutterstock
p.1: Lancaster Castle, acrylic painting by Penny Cameron
p.2: Statue of John O'Gaunt, used by kind permission of the Duchy of Lancaster
p.3: The Gatehouse, photograph by Colin Penny, used by kind permission of the Duchy of Lancaster
p.3: Portcullis mechanism, photograph by Graham Kemp, used by kind permission of the Duchy of Lancaster
p.4: Murder holes, photograph by Colin Penny, used by kind permission of the Duchy of Lancaster
p.4: Military archer, Shutterstock
p.5: Coin bag, Shutterstock
p.5: An illustration of a room in the Gatehouse, engraving by Thomas Physick after a drawing by Edward Slack, used by kind permission of Lancashire County Council Museum Service
p.6: Escape kit, photo by Colin Penny, used by kind permission of Lancashire County Council Museum Service
p.7: The castle courtyard: photograph by Penny Cameron, used by kind permission of the Duchy of Lancaster
p.8: Illustration of the courtyard in 1824 by James Weetman, used by kind permission of Lancaster City Museum
p.8: The castle courtyard, photograph by Penny Cameron, used by kind permission of the Duchy of Lancaster.
p.9: Keys, drawing by Ann-Marie Michel
p.9: Victorian gentleman, Shutterstock
pp.9, 71: Speech bubble, Shutterstock
p.10: The Governor's house, photograph by Colin Penny, used by kind permission of the Duchy of Lancaster
p.11: Roses, Shutterstock
p.11: Watering can, Shutterstock
p.11: Garden fork, Shutterstock
p.12: Witches' Tower, photograph by Colin Penny, used by kind permission of the Duchy of Lancaster
p.13: The steps to the dungeon in the Witches' Tower, used by kind permission of the Duchy of Lancaster
p.13: Well image, Shutterstock
p.13: Robert Bruce, Shutterstock
p.14: Dungeon photo, Carnegie Publishing, used by kind permission of the Duchy of Lancaster
p.14: Candle drawing, Ann-Marie Michel
p.15: Iron ring on the dungeon floor, photograph by Colin Penny, used by kind permission of the Duchy of Lancaster
p.15: Debtors room Illustration, engraving by Thomas Physick after a drawing by Edward Slack, used by kind permission of Lancashire County Council Museum Service
p.16: Designs for the proposed King's Evidence Tower, Lancaster Castle (section), credit RIBA Collections
p.17: King's Evidence Tower, photograph by Colin Penny, used by kind permission of the Duchy of Lancaster
p.17: Detective, Shutterstock
p.17: Cash, Shutterstock
p.18: Noose, Shutterstock

p.18: Pickpockets illustration, Wiki, public domain
p.19: King's Evidence Tower, photograph by Colin Penny, used by kind permission of the Duchy of Lancaster
p.20: The Male Felons' Tower, photograph by Colin Penny, used by kind permission of the Duchy of Lancaster
p.21: Governor Higgin, drawing by Ivan Frontani
p.21: Rat, drawing by Ann-Marie Michel
p.21: Cells inside the Male Felons' Tower, photograph by Colin Penny, used by kind permission of the Duchy of Lancaster
p.22: The Keep, photograph by Colin Penny, used by kind permission of the Duchy of Lancaster
p.23: Early medieval knight on horseback, Shutterstock
p.23: Roger de Poitou stained glass, Wiki, public domain
pp.24–25: The Keep, double-page spread, watercolour by Robert Freebairn, used by kind permission of Lancaster City Museum
p.26: Lancaster from the Moor, from *The Illustrated London News*, public domain
p.27: Inside the Keep: photograph by Colin Penny, used by kind permission of the Duchy of Lancaster
p.28 Warrior with axe, Shutterstock
p28: Castle doorway, drawing by Ann-Marie Michel
p.29: Rocks falling, Shutterstock
p.29: Fire, Shutterstock
pp. 30–31: Convicts exercising at Pentonville Prison, Henry Mayhew, John Binny, and Benno Loewy, *The Criminal Prisons of London and Scenes of Prison Life* (London: Griffin, Bohn, 1862), public domain
p.32: Zipper emoticon, Shutterstock
p.30: Shot drill balls, photograph by Colin Penny, used by kind permission of Lancashire County Council Museum Service
p.33: Prison illustration, State Library of Victoria (Australia)
p.33: Silence Mask, State Library of Victoria (Australia), ©Ciell
p.34: The Debtors' Prison, photograph by Colin Penny, used by kind permission of the Duchy of Lancaster

p.35: Debtor illustration: engraving by Thomas Physick after a drawing by Edward Slack, used by kind permission of Lancashire County Council Museum Service
p.35: Gold coins, Shutterstock
p.36: Penniless man cartoon, Shutterstock
p.37: The Quaker Room, engraving by Thomas Physick after a drawing by Edward Slack, used by kind permission of Lancaster City Museum
p.38: Tankard, Shutterstock
p.38: Antique glass, Shutterstock
p.39: Debtor engraving by Thomas Physick after a drawing by Edward Slack, used by kind permission of Lancashire County Council Museum Service
p.40: The Female Penitentiary, photograph by Colin Penny, used by kind permission of the Duchy of Lancaster
p.41: Cells in the Female Penitentiary, photo by Colin Penny, used by kind permission of the Duchy of Lancaster
p.42: The Female Penitentiary, photograph by Colin Penny, used by kind permission of the Duchy of Lancaster
p43: Ordnance Survey Plan of Lancaster Castle, 1845. Reproduced with permission of the National Library of Scotland
p.44: The Crank, drawing by Ivan Frontani, used by kind permission of Lancashire County Council Museum Service
p.45: Treadmill, Wiki, public domain
p.46: Marsden's loom, Wiki, public domain
p.47: Treadwheel, drawing by Ivan Frontani, used by kind permission of Lancashire County Council Museum Service
p.48: Spider's web, Shutterstock
p.48: Oakum, Shutterstock
p.49: Women picking oakum in the Workhouse, 1900–1919, The National Archives
p.50: Dietary poster, used by kind permission of Lancashire County Council Museum Service
p.51: Cheese, Shutterstock
p.51: Fly, Shutterstock
p.52: Potatoes, Shutterstock

p.52 Boiling pan by Ann-Marie Michel
p.53: Maggot, Shutterstock
p.53, Magnifying glass, Shutterstock
p.54: Hadrian's Tower, photograph by Colin Penny, used by kind permission of Lancashire County Council Museum Service
p.55: King John illustration, Wiki, public domain
p.56: Hadrian's Tower, photograph by Colin Penny, used by kind permission of Lancashire County Council Museum Service
p.57: Hadrian's Tower, photograph by Colin Penny, used by kind permission of Lancashire County Council Museum Service
p.57: Scold's Bridle, photograph by Colin Penny, used by kind permission of Lancashire County Council Museum Service
p.58: Manacles in Hadrian's Tower, photograph by Colin Penny, used by kind permission of Lancashire County Council Museum Service
p.59: Prison Ship Prince of Wales, Wiki, public domain
p.60: Manacles in Hadrian's Tower used to transport convicts, photograph by Colin Penny, used by kind permission of Lancashire County Council Museum Service
p.61: HMS *Neptune*, Wiki, public domain
p.62: Interior of one of the old cells, photograph by Colin Penny, used by kind permission of Lancashire County Council Museum Service
p.63: Cell, Shutterstock
p.64: Dayroom outside the old cells, photograph by Colin Penny, used by kind permission of Lancashire County Council Museum Service
p.65: Hammock, drawing by Ann-Marie Michel
p.65: Gunpowder, Shutterstock
p.66: The Shire Hall canopy, photograph by Colin Penny, used by kind permission of Lancashire County Council Museum Service
p.67: The Shire Hall (external), Wiki/Geograph, public domain
p.68: The Shire Hall, photographs by Colin Penny/Carnegie Publishing, used by kind permission of Lancashire County Council Museum Service
p.69: The Shire Hall: photograph by Colin Penny, used by kind permission of Lancashire County Council Museum Service
p.70: The Shire Hall ceiling, photograph by Colin Penny, used by kind permission of Lancashire County Council Museum Service
p.70: Fordyce shield, drawing by Ann-Marie Michel
p.71: Shield, Carnegie Publishing
p.72: Library, photograph by Colin Penny, used by kind permission of Lancashire County Council Museum Service
p.73: Judge's wig, drawing by Ann-Marie Michel
p.73: Judge's gavel, Shutterstock
p.74: The Library ceiling, photograph by Colin Penny, used by kind permission of Lancashire County Council Museum Service
p.74: Woodworm, iStock photos
p.74: Ambrose Barlow skull, courtesy of Diocese of Salford for Wardley
p.75: Edmund Arrowsmith hand, courtesy of Archdiocese of Liverpool
p.75: Lancashire Martyrs Commemorative Plaque, photograph by Colin Penny, used by kind permission of the Duchy of Lancaster
p.76: Chattox and Redfern: Wiki, public domain
p.76: Pins, Shutterstock
p.76: Frog, Shutterstock
p.76: Witch's hat, drawing by Ann-Marie Michel
p.77: Pendle Witches illustration by Ivan Frontani, Carnegie Publishing.
p.78: The Crown Court, Colin Penny, used by kind permission of Lancashire County Council Museum
p.79: Hand, drawing by Ann-Marie Michel
p.79: Crown image, Shutterstock
p.80: Portrait of George III, Colin Penny, used by kind permission of Lancashire County Council Museum Service
p.80: Branding iron, Carnegie Publishing, used by kind permission of Lancashire County Council Museum Service

119

p.81: Crown Court illustration, artist unknown, used by kind permission of Lancashire County Council Museum Service
p.81: A Calendar of Crown Prisoners, used by kind permission of Lancashire County Council Museum Service
p.82: Hangman's noose, photograph by Colin Penny, used by kind permission of Lancashire County Council Museum Service
p.83: Lancaster from the Moor, from *The Illustrated London News*, public domain
p.83: Pinioning strap, Carnegie Publishing, used by kind permission of Lancashire County Council Museum Service
p.84: The Drop Room, Carnegie Publishing, used by kind permission of Lancashire County Council Museum Service
p.85: Hanging Corner, photograph by Colin Penny, used by kind permission of Lancashire County Council Museum Service
p.86: Queen Victoria's throne, photograph by Colin Penny, used by kind permission of Lancashire County Council Museum Service
p.87: The Grand Jury Room, photograph by Colin Penny, used by kind permission of Lancashire County Council Museum Service
p.87: John Higgin, drawing by Ann-Marie Michel
p.88: The Grand Jury Room, photograph by Colin Penny, used by kind permission of Lancashire County Council Museum Service
p.88: Gillow chair heads, photograph by Colin Penny, used by kind permission of Lancashire County Council Museum Service
p.89: The Grand Jury Room ceiling, photograph by Colin Penny, used by kind permission of Lancashire County Council Museum Service
p.90: The Duchy of Lancaster flag, photo by Colin Penny, used by kind permission of the Duchy of Lancaster
p.91: King Henry IV Coat of Arms, photograph by Colin Penny, used by kind permission of Lancashire County Council Museum Service
p.91: Crown, Shutterstock
p.91: Henry IV, Wiki, public domain
p.93: The Duchy of Lancaster castles, used by kind permission of the Duchy of Lancaster
p.94: The Gatehouse, Carnegie Publishing, used by kind permission of the Duchy of Lancaster
p.95: The Shire Hall (exterior), used by kind permission of the Duchy of Lancaster
p.95 German military helmet, Shutterstock
p.96: German war graves, photograph by Ann-Marie Michel
p.96: Cartoon cop and robber, Shutterstock
p.97: ROC pin and cap badges, used by kind permission of Lancashire County Council Museum Service
p.97: Spitfire toppling V-1, by Walton, CH16281, Imperial War Museums collection, public domain
p.97: Dove, Shutterstock
p.98: Tourists, Shutterstock
p.99: Queen, Shutterstock
p.99: Shakespeare, Shutterstock
p.100: Wych Elm, Penny Cameron, Carnegie Publishing
p.101: Castle Hill, Penny Cameron, Carnegie Publishing
p.102: Higgin portrait, James Sant RA, private collection
p.103: John Higgin drawing by Ann-Marie Michel
p.105: Castle courtyard, photograph by Colin Penny, used by kind permission of the Duchy of Lancaster
p.109: Weather vane, photograph by Colin Penny, used by kind permission of the Duchy of Lancaster
p.110: Courtyard view, photo by Martin Stone. Used by courtesy of the Duchy of Lancaster
p.114: Male Felons' and King's Evidence Towers, photo by Martin Stone, used by kind permission of the Duchy of Lancaster